Maximizing Your Mini Farm

How to Create a Sustainable Organic Garden in Your Backyard You Can Be Proud Of (Square Foot Gardening, Small Space Gardening, Mini Farming For Beginners)

Louann Ransdell

Overview of Mini-Farming

Mini-farming differs primarily in its lack of focus on growing grains from the Grow Biointensive process, but it also dispenses with the methods of seed starting and plant spacing, among others. Mini-farming differs from the Biodynamic approach in that it does not use specific herbal preparations to prepare fertilizer, plant seeds by phases of the moon, or find the farm to be an object of its own making. There are so many other variations, you can't count them all. This mini-farming approach differs from the French Intensive system in that it does not rely on large inputs of manure from horses. The French approach is similar to Grow Biointensive in many respects and these variations also apply.

Intensive farming practices are being continuously perfected, extended, updated and developed by well-known practitioners and individual farmers. Agriculture is at its heart a method which is more biological than industrial. As a result, it is subject to the rules of nature that we humans only begin to understand. As with any other endeavor, the path to success of intensive agriculture is through continuously growing knowledge.

You're expected to have journals every year. One journal lists each plant variety to be grown in the year in which the seed was acquired, and general information on the plant and its requirements. This is accompanied by journal entries explaining where, when and how the seeds were started; details on the transplantation of seeds; and significant events that affected the crop through harvesting. Any pest problems are reported in the article, along with the efficacy of any solutions and, in particular, details that might provide a clue as to why certain plants of a given crop might have been more or less affected.

Plant spacing is another significant journal entry unique to intensive agriculture. The starting value for the two-dimensional plant spacing is the in-row thinning distance defined in the seed set. This will provide optimal yields in a row-type system and will often yield optimum yields in a raised-bed intensive system, although a small amount of experimentation is in order, as yields relative to spacing will differ with soil and climate conditions. In the case of lettuce in my own yard, I have found that eight-inch spaces perform better than six-inch spaces — but the results will be different for different soils and climates.

Journals are an important resource for learning and developing. All this knowledge helps to fine-tune the climate that I offer to the plant from year to year so that my reliance on fertilizers, horse manure and other external inputs — even organic — can be minimized from year to year. A journal of crop-specific knowledge also lets me determine whether or not I want to grow a particular crop variety next year, or maybe grow it differently.

Another log to be held is a list of weather events, especially anomalies or anything that affects crops. This journal helps you to know that, in my field, you need to protect young spinach plants from hail when they are planted before the last frost date. Having this information in hand enables my crops to be more competitive and to suffer less harm. You also keep a calendar / planner that lets me lay down during the year when I need to perform different tasks — such as starting and transplanting seedlings or harvesting green manures. Such a calendar helps me to see and focus on labor bottlenecks in advance.

Note in the planner the date of the first harvests for each crop on the basis of the reported maturity dates for the crops, and you should take note of the instances where a particular crop matured sooner or later than expected. Predicted harvest dates often allow me to see in advance when succession planting or starting a crop at a time when it would not usually be used to minimize peak food preservation workloads so that work can be better spread out.

The final journal lists basically everything I do about soil fertility, including digging beds, compost material, soil organic changes, crop rotations, and so on. This knowledge is combined with knowledge on crop production and insect or disease problems.

The purpose behind all this journaling is to place all the interactions and findings in a sense that helps me to use this knowledge effectively to make better decisions every year than in the previous year. Working with biological systems is a cycle of continuous learning, and in the end, a mini-farmer will benefit from holding comprehensive notes. Intensive agriculture, since it grows plants close together in a fairly small area of land, is a field with plenty of space for exploration and makes the results of the experiment more readily apparent to the farmer. This gives mini-farmers the ability to make technological progress much faster than those involved in industrial farming.

Chapter One
Pest and disease control

Pest and disease problems are an unavoidable fact of life for the mini-farmer. Sometimes, they are barely noticeable and cause no significant problems. But at other times they can cause major crop losses. There are, unfortunately, hundreds of pests and diseases that affect vegetable crops. Active prevention is used when experience or reliable data indicate that a particular pest or disease is likely to be a problem. Active reaction is employed when the value of likely crop damage will exceed the costs of active reaction methods. Passive prevention is the application of good farming practices: well-composted and appropriately amended healthy soil, adequate sunshine, proper watering, crop rotation, and sufficient airflow.

In essence, this simply means to give plants growing conditions that are as close to optimal as possible. This will make them healthier and thus less susceptible to diseases and less attractive to pests. Active prevention uses active measures to prevent diseases or repel insect pests. Examples include applying repellent garlic or hot pepper sprays on plants to deter pests, installing physical barriers, putting out traps, or spraying the plants periodically with a fungus preventative. Sometimes, for certain types of pests, poisons that are usually used as a reactive measure may be required as active prevention. Active reaction occurs when preventative measures fail and a problem already exists. Active reaction will often employ the same methods as active prevention, only with greater intensity, but it will also include, in most cases, the application of natural botanical or synthetic poisons or fungicides.

Pest management needs to be viewed holistically, as part of a bigger picture, to minimize crop damage while simultaneously protecting the long-range viability of the mini-farm. As part of this view, it is good to establish a threshold for what constitutes an acceptable level of damage before reactive, as opposed to preventative, measures need to be taken. This threshold is established economically, considering that the time, costs, and risks associated with active pest control measures will diminish the net grocery savings. So the threshold of acceptable damage for a given crop, in terms of percentage crop loss, is the level at which the value of the lost crop portion exceeds the cost of active control measures.

Potato beetles are a common garden pest.

Passive Prevention

Passive prevention gives the biggest bang for both your time and money because the focus lies mainly in performing ordinary farming chores. Soil, water, sunshine, and crop rotations are the foundation of pest and disease control; all of these create an environment inhospitable to the persistence of pests and disease. A healthy, living soil with plenty of nutrients allows for vigorous growth so that crops can outgrow problems. In addition, healthier plants are less attractive to pests and less susceptible to disease in most cases. Healthy soil plays host to various portions of the life cycles of many beneficial insect populations, along with beneficial microbes that compete with nasty pathogens for nutrients and generate antibiotics to eliminate them. It is no mistake that forests thrive independent of human intervention, and the more closely a farmer's garden approximates naturally optimal conditions for a crop, the less susceptible it will be to pest and disease problems. An important aspect of healthy soil, particularly with intensive agriculture, is compost. As discussed in chapter 5, merely using compost in your soil can significantly reduce pest and disease problems. Proper watering is another important aspect of disease control.

Plant diseases spread most easily when plant tissues are wet; both excessive watering and overhead watering can increase the likelihood of disease problems. However, adequate moisture is also important because drought-stressed plants become more attractive to pests. Crop rotation is impossible to over emphasize. Just like there are viruses and bacteria that affect some mammals but not others—such as feline leukemia—there are numerous plant diseases that affect one family of vegetables but not others. Since these microbes need a host hospitable to their reproduction to complete their life cycles, depriving them of the host they need through crop rotation is extremely effective at controlling many diseases. The same applies to insect pests, so the same crop should not be grown in the samebed two years in a row. Ideally, crop rotation will prevent crops of the same family from growing in the same bed any more often than once every three years. Specific plant variety selection is another important preventative. Notwithstanding the economic benefits of using open-pollinated seeds (described in the next chapter), some hybrids carry diseaseand pest-resistance genes that can make them a better choice if certain diseases or pests become a repetitive problem. On my farm, for example, I now grow hybrid cucumbers that are resistant to bacterial wilt disease. Dill is a common attractant of beneficial insects.

Finally, never discount the power of the sun. The same UV rays that make excessive sunshine a risk factor for skin cancer also scramble the genetic code in bacteria and viruses, rendering them incapable of infection. Sunshine sanitizes. Attracting beneficial insects is also useful. Most beneficial insects feed on or invade pest species at some point in their life cycle, but they also require certain plants for their well-being. Providing these plants in the garden will give beneficial insects a base of operations they can use to keep pest species controlled. A small planting of early, intermediate season, and late-blooming beneficial insect attractors in each garden bed will help stack the deck in the farmer's favor. Ladybugs love to eat aphids; dandelion, marigold, and hairy vetch will attract them. Tachanid flies help keep cabbage worms and stink bugs in check; a planting of parsley or pennyroyal will give them a home.

Beneficial insect attractors that bloom early include sweet alyssum, columbine, and creeping thyme. Intermediate bloomers include common yarrow, cilantro, edging lobelia, and mints. Late bloomers include dill, wild bergamot, and European goldenrod. An easy plan is to plant a few marigolds throughout the bed, a columbine plant, a bit of cilantro, and some dill. You should familiarize yourself with the properties of beneficial plant attractors before planting them in your beds. Don't just run out

Preventative Plantings Beneficial Insect

Controlled Pests

Plants to Provide

Parasitic wasps

Moth, beetle, and fly larvae and eggs, including caterpillars

Dill, yarrow, tansy, Queen Anne's lace, parsley

Hoverflies (syrphid flies)

Mealybugs, aphids As

above, plus marigold

Lacewings

Aphids, mealybugs, other small insects

Dandelion, angelica, dill, yarrow

Ladybugs

Aphids

Dandelion, hairy vetch, buckwheat, marigold

Tachanid flies

Caterpillars, cabbage loopers, stink bugs, cabbage bugs, beetles,
Parsley, tansy, pennyroyal, buckwheat and plant mint in the
garden bed directly, for example, because it will take over the
entire bed. Instead, plant mint in a pot and then bury the pot in
the garden soil so that the upper edge sticks out of the soil 1/2
inch or so. You may also want to choose some plants that you
will already use in some other way—such as mint for tea, dill for
pickling, and cilantro for salsa. That way you are making
maximum use of limited space. There is nothing wrong with
growing goldenrods just because they are pretty! Another
valuable addition to the garden and yard, once the seeds have
sprouted and the plants are growing well, would be chickens or
guineas. Both types of birds, but guineas particularly, wreak
havoc on bugs, especially bugs like ticks that nobody wants
around anyway. Such livestock can effectively keep many sorts
of garden pests from reaching the critical mass of population
necessary to be threatening to crops.

Active Prevention

Active prevention is often necessary when a particular pest or disease problem is a practical certainty. In such cases, the active prevention is tailored to the expected problem and can often encompass methods used for both passive prevention and intervention. For example, you may notice your garden is regularly infested with earwigs. Once the bugs are noticed inside a cauliflowerplant, they've already done a lot of damage. A weekly spraying with pyrethrin (a natural insecticide) or hot pepper wax (a repellent) will increase the usable harvest significantly. The materials and techniques most often used for active prevention include traps, immune boosters, compost extracts, imported beneficial insects, and application of repellents, fungicides, and pesticides. (The latter is particularly important with certain fruit trees.)

Lures and Traps

Many insect pests can be caught in traps. In commercial operations, traps are usually used to monitor pest populations to determine the optimal timing for the application of pesticides. In a mini-farm, because of the smaller land area involved, it is often practical to employ enough traps to completely eradicate a particular pest (or one of the sexes of that pest) in the garden without resorting to poisons. Examples of pests easily trapped are codling moths, Japanese beetles, and apple maggots. Traps can also be employed for cucumber beetles, white flies, and a number of other pests, but they tend to be less effective. The time when various insects emerge varies from area to area. Because the lures used in traps often have limited lifespan, the timing of their deployment can be important. This is something you'll learn from keeping notes, and within a couple of years you'll have no trouble with the timing of traps.

Immunity Boosters and Growth Enhancers

One immune booster for plants on the market at the moment is marketed by Eden Bioscience in the form of harpin protein. Harpin protein, which is produced naturally by the bacterium that causes fire blight in apples and pears, elicits a broad immune response from vegetables that makes them more resistant to a wide array of pests and diseases while enhancing their growth. Eden Bioscience

uses this discovery in a product called Messenger that is nontoxic and relatively inexpensive at my local agricultural supply store. A company called Vitamin Institute sells a product called Superthrive that is advertised to improve the growth rate of plants and whose primary ingredient is thiamine. I have done some sideby-side testing, and the results have been ambiguous. On the other hand, I have found a growth enhancer called Root

Boost to live up to its advertising. It is not a fertilizer but rather an enhancer that is primarily based on kelp extract with the addition of humic acids. This product, when used as directed, really does enhance the soil and the plants that depend on it.

Compost Extract and Compost

Tea Compost extract is the most well-known and most widely studied homemade disease preventative. It is exactly what it sounds like: a shovel of properly aged compost in a water-permeable sack immersed in a bucket of water and steeped for 7 to 14 days. As the chapter on composting pointed out, compost extract contains a cocktail of microbes and the chemicals that they produce. Compost extract contains a mix of beneficial bacteria and fungi that, when sprayed onto plants, eats the food substances that would otherwise be eaten by disease-causing organisms. As a result, the disease-causing organisms get starved out.

A biweekly spray of compost extract is a good idea, and numerous studies attribute properties to the substance that are nothing short of miraculous. It can help prevent diseases such as black spot and powdery mildew. Best of all, it's free. The next step up from compost extract is compost tea. Compost tea differs from an extract in that it is the result of an active attempt to increase the amount of fungi and bacteria in the solution through aeration. Still water (as used in compost extract) doesn't have much dissolved oxygen in it, and the beneficial microbes in compost require oxygen. So, actively aerating the water in which the compostis steeped will serve to boost populations of beneficial microbes from the compost. This can be done inexpensively by putting a fish tank aerator and air pump in the bottom of a container containing the water and compost.

Importing Beneficial Insects and Nematodes

Imported beneficial insects have their greatest applicability in greenhouses because, being quite mobile, when applied outdoors they are prone to fly away. Even outside they can be useful though, particularly when applied to crops infested with their favorite pest species and also provided with their favorite plants.

Beneficial nematodes are extremely small worms that wait underground for a chance to work their way into pest insects and kill them. Beneficial nematodes are harmless to plants and pollinators and shouldn't be confused with pest nematodes such as root knot nematodes. Once inside the host, the nematodes release their gut bacteria, Xenorhabdusluminescens, into the insect's interior, where the bacteria multiply and the nematodes feed on them. The pest species eventually dies from infection. There are two commonly used species of nematodes. Beneficial nematode products often contain both species to be as broadly useful as possible. Beneficial nematodes require extreme care in their handling and are usually shipped by overnight courier in a refrigerated package. They are stored in the refrigerator until they are used. It is best to wait until ground temperatures are above 50 degrees, the ground is damp, and a light rain is falling. Then put the nematodes in a pump-style sprayer and apply them to the ground where you wantthem. The reason for this is that beneficial nematodes are very prone to dehydration, and the falling rain helps them get into the soil. If you live north of Maryland, you'll need to apply them yearly because they can't survive the winter. If you live in a more southerly clime, the nematodes will probably survive, so a second application may not be needed.

Beneficial Nematodes Species

Pests Controlled

Steinernemaspp

Webworms, cutworms, vine borers

Heterorhabditisspp

White grubs, vine weevils, root weevils

Notes Not effective against grubs

Pest Repellents Organic repellent mixtures are not 100% effective, but they serve as a valuable part of an integrated strategy for pest management. One repellent mixture is simple hot pepper. Capsaicin, the active ingredient in hot peppers, repels onion, carrot, and cabbage maggots. Simply finely chop up a cup of hot peppers, and steep it for a day in a gallon of water to which a single drop of dish soap has been added. Another repellent mixture is garlic, manufactured the same way. One thing that I do, with great success, is make hot pepper and garlic mixtures in a coffee maker that has been set aside for agricultural use only. There are some commercial repellent preparations worth noting as well, including CropGuard and Hot Pepper Wax. There is some evidence that certain plants can repel pest insects.

According to numerous sources, for example, nasturtiums and radishes repel cucumber beetles. I have experimented extensively with this practice and found no difference in cucumber beetle populations between cucumber plants surrounded by radishes and intertwined with nasturtiums and cucumber plants grown on their own. On the other hand, I have found that onion family crops repel wireworms, so I interplant leeks with my parsnips. A number of sites on the Internet list repellent plants, so I encourage you to experiment with the reputed properties of repellent plants and keep notes to see what works best for your garden.

Active Reaction

Even the most conscientious farming practices and most vigilant preventive measures will often fail to prevent pest and disease problems. Once these problems become apparent, reactive measures are in order. Reactive measures will often include some of the same materials and methods as passive and active prevention. For example, many fungal infections can be eradicated by the timely application of compost tea, neem oil, or garlic oil. (Neem oil is an oil extracted from a tree in India.) Most often, though, reactive measures will involve the use of fungicides and/or natural or synthetic pesticides. Because these reactive measures use substances with greater potential to harm people or the environment, I don't recommend their application unless the farmer is certain that a likelihood exists that failure to apply them will result in an unacceptable level of crop loss. Another tip to make active measures most effective is to take a cue from doctors treating HIV and tuberculosis: Never treat aninsect or disease problem with only one active agent at a time. Using only one active agent increases the odds of survivors living to convey immunity to that agent in the next generation. When you mix two or more active agents, you increase the odds of success while decreasing the odds of creating resistant organisms. So, for example, I routinely apply pyrethrin and rotenone in tandem, neem oil mixed with a microbial insecticide, or garlic and hot pepper repellents mixed together.

When Disease Prevention Fails Plant diseases fall into four broad categories: bacterial, viral, protozoan, and fungal. Usually, these are impossible to distinguish by the naked eye except through experience with their symptoms. (See also the Rodale book recommended earlier in this chapter.) All such diseases present the problem that once a plant is infected, it becomes a storehouse of infective particles that can be spread to other plants via insects, wind, or handling. The longer an affected plant remains in the garden, the greater the odds that it will infect other plants. Diseases caused by viruses, bacteria, and protozoans are seldom treatable, but sometimes you can save a plant by pruning out the affected portions.

Many fungal diseases, though, are treatable through a combination of pruning and spraying. When a plant infection of any sort is first noticed, you may be able to save the plant by applying compost tea and/or Messenger. These products can stimulate an immune response that helps the plant overcome the infection. Their usefulness in that regard varies depending on the plants and diseases involved, so try it and keep notes of the results. A number of spray fungicides can also be used. Common fungicides include copper sulfate, Bordeaux mix (a mixture of copper sulfate and lime), baking soda, garlic oil, and neem oil. Baking soda is mixed two tablespoons per gallon of water with one ounce of light horticultural oil added, and the others are mixed according to label directions. Some less well-known antifungal agents can have surprising

results. I had a problem with powdery mildew on my lawn last spring (we had an especially wet spring), and I eliminated the infection by spraying with a mix of neem oil and fixed copper. If saving the plant is either unsuccessful or inadvisable, then the plant should be removed from the garden immediately. Removing an infectious plant can be problematic since it can be covered with microscopic spores that will spread all over the place if the plant is disturbed.

The solution is to spray the plant with something that will hold any spores in place and inactivate as many as possible before attempting removal. A good spray for this is made of two tablespoons of castile soap, one tablespoon of copper sulfate, one tablespoon of lime, and one tablespoon of light horticultural oil all mixed together in a gallon of water. The soap and oil will make the plant sticky so that spores can't escape, while the copper sulfate and lime serve to actually kill many infectious organisms. Spray the plant thoroughly with this (though not until it is dripping), and then cut it out and remove it, being as careful as possible to avoid letting it touch any other plants.

When dealing with plant diseases, you should consider your hands and tools to be a mode of disease transmission.

When handling known diseased plants, it makes sense to handle only the diseased plants before hand washing and also to immediately sterilize any tools used on the diseased plants with bleach. A suitable sanitizing solution is one tablespoon of bleach per quart of water. Diseased plant materials can be thermophilically composted with minimal or no risk as long as proper retention times are observed. If the farmer uses mesophilic composting instead, then diseased plant debris should be burned or placed in the curbside trash. It is also very important not to grow the same family of plant in the same area the next year. If a variety of the plant that resists that disease can be found, it would be a good idea to switch to that variety for at least a year or two, if not permanently.

When Pest Prevention Fails

The best soil management and prevention mechanisms will not be 100% effective against insect pests. For example, naturally attracted beneficial insects exist in balance with pest insects. If the beneficial insects were to eat all of the pest species, then the beneficial insects would starve or move somewhere else, and the pest species would experience a resurgence in the absence of its natural enemies.

Reactive control measures include anything used in the preventive stages, along with importing beneficial insect populations, applying microbial insecticides, and using substances that actually kill insects directly, such as soaps, oils, and natural or synthetic insecticides. Synthetic insecticides should be reserved as a last resort since they would reduce the healthfulness of the crop and would make it impossible for you to sell your produce as organic for several years if you wish to do so. Both natural and artificial insecticides can also harm beneficial helpers, such as necessary pollinators and earthworms, and disrupt the life of the soil and thus harm fertility in the long run, so they are best employed only when absolutely necessary. Because natural insecticides don't last as long in the garden, they have less potential to do unintended damage.

Microbial Insecticides

Microbial insecticides are microbes (or toxins produced by microbes) that are deadly to pest insects but harmless to beneficial insects and humans. They have the advantage of being relatively benign but the disadvantage of being fairly species specific. For example, Bacillus popilliae is deadly to Japanese beetle larvae but harmless to other white grubs that infest lawns. They aren't contact poisons, and they must be eaten by the insect to be effective. Microbial insecticides have become increasingly popular, even among conventional farmers, and are readily available at agriculturalstores.

Soaps and Oils Plain old soap (not detergent, but soap) kills a number of insects by dissolving a waxy coating that they need to breathe and preserve moisture. Specialized insecticidal soaps can be used, or else a pure castile soap, mixed two tablespoons per gallon of water. Insecticidal soap will effectively control aphids, white

Common Microbial Insecticides Microbe

Bacillus thuringiensis var. kurstaki

The caterpillar stage of a wide variety of moths

Will not control codling moths

Bacillus thuringiensis var. israelensis

Mosquito, black fly, fungus gnat

Bacillus thuringiensis var. san diego

Colorado potato beetle

Nosema locustae

Grasshoppers

Because of grasshopper mobility, may not work for small yards
flies, scale, spider mites, and thrips. It needs to be reapplied
fairly frequently—about weekly—to interrupt the life cycle of the
target pest. Light horticultural oils are highly refined mineral
oils that control the same insects as insecticidal soap by covering
and smothering the pest and its eggs. Mix and apply according
to label directions. Both oils and soaps should be tested on a
single plant first, then wait a day, because they can be toxic to
certain plants. (Their degree of toxicity to plants varies with
heat, sunshine, humidity, general plant health, and other
factors. Most often, they won't cause a problem, but it never
hurts to test first.)

Natural Insecticides

The fact that something is natural doesn't mean that it is
harmless. Ebola, smallpox, and strychnine are all 100% natural,
for example. Natural insecticides fall under the same category
and thus require care in their use. Natural insecticides can be
purchased, or they can be grown and made at home. From a cost
standpoint, the latter approach is preferable, though certain
natural insecticides aren't practical for home manufacture.

Pyrethrin is a contact insecticide that controls most aphids, cabbage loopers, stinkbugs, codling moths, and white flies among other pests. It does not affect flea beetles, imported cabbage worms, or tarnished plant bugs.

To make your own pyrethrin, grow pyrethrum daisies (Tanacetumcinerarifolium) somewhere in the garden. Cut the flowers when they are in full bloom for the highest concentration of poison, and hang them upside down in a cool, dry, dark place to dry. Once they are dried, take a quart jar of the dried flowers and grind them up using an old food processor or blender that you pick up at a yard sale and that you will never use for food again. Mix it with one gallon ofwater and two drops of dish liquid, and allow it to steep for three days, stirring every once in a while. When done, filter it through cheese cloth that you will throw away afterward, store in a tightly capped bottle in a cool dark place, and label it appropriately as a poison so nobody drinks it accidentally.

You dilute this for use by mixing one quart of the poison with three quarts of water, shaking, and applying via a sprayer. (I cannot stress strongly enough that all bottles containing poisons of any sort be labeled appropriately. Not far from where I live, a child died tragically a couple of years ago because of an unlabeled container of insecticide.) Other natural insecticides are widely available, including neem and rotenone. These can be purchased at most garden centers or via mail order and should be used with as much care and caution as synthetics, because they can be toxic to humans.

Synthetic Pesticides While this book focuses on organic methods, synthetic pesticides available to home gardeners bear mentioning. Ideally, because of a combination of growing conditions, attraction of natural predators, and other factors, pests won't be a problem so no pesticides will be needed—synthetic or otherwise. But that's the ideal. Reality can be far different, especially when first beginning a mini-farm. Even the most careful planning won't completely eliminate pest problems.

As a mini-farmer, you are trying to put a lot of food on the table, and you are trying to put safe food on the table. Perhaps, like me, you are an organic purist. But what happens when the theory of being an organic purist runs into the reality of a pest problem that threatens an entire crop? In my case, since I sell my produce as organic at 200% higher rates than conventional produce, it is actually better for me to lose a crop entirely than use synthetic pesticides. But what if my operation were strictly oriented toward putting food on the table? In that case, maybe I would use them, albeit cautiously and as a last resort, because some research shows that the synthetic pesticides available at the hardware store can be just as safe as botanical insecticides—and more effective—when used properly. Please note that I said "maybe," "cautiously," and "as a last resort" for a reason. First off, in a mini-farm established using the methods in this book, economically threatening insect problems should be rare, and insect problems that won't respond to natural remedies even more rare. In fact, I have had only one pest problem where synthetics would have possibly been the better short-term solution.

Second, the government agencies charged with ensuring the safety of foodstuffs, drugs, and insecticides have a poor track record. For example, an article in USA Today disclosed that in 55% of FDA meetings regarding drug approvals, over half of the participants had financial conflicts of interest serious enough to note.27 According to the same article, committees approving such things are actually required by law to include officials representing the industry in question. This is not exactly a recipe that would inspire confidence in most objective observers and perhaps explains the dozens of chemicals (including various insecticides and drugs) approved by government agencies and subsequently recalled after people have been harmed or killed.

Finally, studies indicate that synthetic pesticides make food less healthful by reducing the ability of plants to create antioxidants.28 This explains my caution regarding synthetic pesticides. If you are nice enough to buy my book, should I repay your kindness by giving you advice that could hurt you without totally disclosing the facts as I know them? Government agencies have a poor track record, and research in universities is often funded by self-interested parties.

The extent to which this affects the results and conclusions of research is impossible to tell. So I am going to give you information on two synthetic insecticides, understanding that the research I have available says they are safe but that it could be discovered later that you shouldn't touch them with the proverbial 10-foot pole. The use of natural insecticides like pyrethrin and rotenone isperfectly acceptable under the National Organic Program, but in practical terms these substances are every bit as toxic as commonly available synthetics while being less effective in many instances. The main difference is that the natural insecticides break down into nontoxic compounds very quickly under the influence of heat, sunshine, wind, and rain so they won't make it into your food supply if used properly, whereas the synthetics are specifically formulated to be more persistent. Let's take pyrethrin as an example.

Pyrethrin is a natural neurotoxin that insects quickly absorb through the skin. Once it is absorbed, the race is on between the insect's enzymes that detoxify the pyrethrin and the pyrethrin's toxic effects. Many insects, if they receive a sublethal dose, will pick themselves up and dust themselves off less than an hour after apparently being killed! Synthetic pyrethrins approach this problem by mixing the product with a substance like piperonylbutoxide that delays the insect's ability to make the enzymes to detoxify the pyrethrin, thus lowering the threshold considerably for what would constitute a lethal dose. Moreover, semisynthetic pyrethrins, such as allethrin, are often more toxic to insects while being less toxic to mammals (such as humans) than their natural counterparts. So a semisynthetic pyrethrin spray combined with piperonylbutoxide would require less poison to be used and be more effective, and the type of pyrethrin being used would be less toxic to humans.

According to a metabolic study, neither natural nor synthetic pyrethrins accumulate in the body or show up in breast milk because they are quickly detoxified in the human body. Any allethrin consumed by a human is rapidly transformed into something less toxic and eliminated. 31 In addition, allethrin is broken down into nontoxic compounds through the action of air and sunlight within a few days,32 though not as quickly as natural pyrethrin. The piperonylbutoxide used to increase the effectiveness of pyrethrins is a semisynthetic derivative of safrole—an oil found in the bark of sassafras trees. It works by inhibiting enzymes that detoxify the pyrethrins in the insect's body. Safrole is a known carcinogen, but the status of piperonylbutoxide as a carcinogen is disputed.

Unlike allethrin, piperonylbutoxide is stable in the environment and doesn't break down easily. Given current information, the allethrin doesn't worry me much, but I am sufficiently uneasy about the persistence of piperonylbutoxide in the environment that I wouldn't personally use it. Either way, synthetic pyrethrins and those containing piperonylbutoxide should be used according to label directions and never be used on crops within a week of harvest; even then harvested crops should be well washed. Carbaryl (also known as "Sevin") is another common synthetic insecticide used in home gardens. There is no clear evidence that carbaryl is carcinogenic or causes birth defects, and 85% of carbaryl is excreted by humans within 24 hours.34 Carbaryl has a half-life of 7 to 14 days in sandy loam soil, and the manufacturer (GardenTech) states that it is not absorbed by the plant.

Therefore, if used according to label directions, and produce is carefully washed, it should be safe. According to numerous studies, "Carbaryl breaks down readily and experience shows it readily decomposes on plants, in soil and water to less toxic byproducts. Accumulation in animal tissues and biomagnification of residues in food chains with carbaryl and its metabolites does not occur."

Certainly, the preponderance of science says that carbaryl is perfectly safe when used according to label directions. It definitely takes care of cucumber beetles much more effectively than my organic approaches. Nevertheless, common sense and the fact that it is a neurotoxin that takes a lot longer than most botanical insecticides to break down would dictate that it be used only as a last resort. All in all, if I were to use a synthetic insecticide, I would use carbaryl in preference to the others available. And, in fact, that is what I used before switching to organic gardening.

Animal Pests

So far, in this chapter, when discussing pests we've largely been talking about insects. But one ignores larger pests, such as raccoons, rabbits, and deer, at his or her farm's peril. For many years, my farm ran along just fine with only minor damage from moles who ate strawberries and ripe tomatoes, and raccoons who occasionally stole an ear of corn. But one year, my entire crop of beans, sweet potatoes, and Brussels sprouts was wiped out in just one night by a herd of hungry deer. And they kept coming back to nibble at the sad remains. Clearly, action was needed.

Moles can be a bit of a nuisance in my garden. They are there, primarily, to eat grubs. If you get rid of the grubs by applying Milky Spore or beneficial nematodes, you will dramatically reduce the mole population. For faster relief, there are a number of castor oil products on the market that put castor oil into the dirt. When the moles dig, they get the castor oil on their fur, and they lick it off. This gives them diarrhea, and they move on

within a couple of weeks. I've found this quite effective. A
number of companies sell a battery-powered spike that
generates noise that is supposed to deter moles. These may work
for you, but I've found them ineffective. Rabbits are only an
occasional problem and don't usually do much damage on the
farm. What I do is mix a hot pepper product with anything else I
happen to be spraying and use it to wet the leaves. This serves as
sufficient deterrent.

Products for deterring furry pests. Deer are another matter entirely. Bars of soap, hair clippings, urinating around the property line, and similar homespun remedies did nothing. Spraying the plants with hot pepper wax was inadequate and only marginally effective. I have found only three things that really work. The first is quite expensive: an impenetrable physical barrier in the form of a fence eight-feet tall. The second is a product called Deer Scram, which is a deterrent scent that is sprinkled around the area to be protected. The third is the use of a baited electric fence. A baited electric fence is a regular electric fence that has been baited with peanut butter wrapped in aluminum foil. Deer adore peanut butter, so they put their mouth right on the aluminum foil and get zapped. This works incredibly well and requires only a single strand of fencing about four feet off the ground where pets are safe. This same trick works for raccoons if you add another strand about 18 inches off the ground.

Chapter Two

Seed starting in Mini-Farming

It is a good idea to learn to start seedlings for three reasons. Thefirst reason is economic: Starting seedlings at home saves money. The second reason is variety: Starting seedlings at home vastly increases the range of crop choices because certain varieties may not be available at your local garden center. Finally, since seedlings grown at home were never in a commercial greenhouse, you'll have a known-good product that is unlikely to be harboring pests. Starting seeds is simple: Place seeds in a fertile starting medium in a suitable container; provide water, heat, and light; and that's it. Many seeds—such as grains and beets—are sowed directly in a garden bed, but others such as tomatoes, broccoli, and peppers, must be either started in advance or purchased as small plants ("seedlings") and then transplanted.

Timing

Seedlings need to be started indoors anywhere from 2 to 12 weeks before transplant time, depending on the particular crop. Transplant time is reckoned in weeks before or after the last predicted frost of the year for spring and summer crops and in weeks before the first predicted frost for fall and winter crops. The timing of transplanting is dictated by the hardiness of the particular crop. Broccoli is pretty hardy, so it is often planted 6 weeks before the last predicted frost, whereas cucumber is very tender, so it is planted 1 or 2 weeks after. So the most important information that you will need for starting seeds is the date of the last frost for your geographic region. This can be found from the Cooperative Extension Service or from an

Internet search in most cases. The National Climatic Data Center maintains comprehensive tables on the Internet that give the statistical likelihoods of frost on a given date along with the probabilities of the number of frost-free days, broken down by state and city. Weather.com also provides data relevant to gardening. Once you've determined the average date of your last spring frost, determine the date for starting seeds and transplanting seedlings into the garden by adding or subtracting a certain number of weeks from the date of the last frost, depending on the crop.

If my average last spring frost is June 1st, then I would start my tomato plants seven weeks before June 1st and set them out on that date. Cabbage would be started 13 weeks before June 1st and set out in the garden 5 weeks before June 1st. Eggplant would be started 8 weeks before June 1st and set out 2 weeks after June 1st. Anything that can be planted in the garden before the last spring frost can also be grown as a fall crop. For fall cabbage, if my average date of the first fall frost is on September 6th, and my cabbage requires 65 days to mature according to the seed package, then I would transplant my cabbage seedlings on July 28th. This is computed by adding 25 days to September 6th then subtracting 65 days for the days to maturity (from the seed package). I can tell when to start my cabbage from seed by subtracting 56 days from the transplant date. So I should start my cabbage seedlings for fall on June 2nd.

Starting Medium

Gardening experts have many varied opinions on the best starting medium. To confuse matters, seed catalogs try to sell allkinds of starting mediums for that purpose, and the number of choices can be confusing. Whatever is used as a seed-starting medium should be light and easy for delicate roots to penetrate, and it should hold water well and not be infected with diseases. It should have some nutrients but not too heavy a concentration of them. Commercial seed-starting mixes are sold for this purpose and work fine, as do peat pellets of various shapes and sizes.

Commercial seedstarting mixes cost about $3 for enough to start 150 plants, and peat pellets cost about $5 per 100. Compared to the cost of buying transplants from a garden center, the price of seed-starting mixes or peat pellets is negligible. But for a farmer growing hundreds or even thousands of transplants, it may be economical to make seed-starting mixes at home.

Most seedstarting mixes consist mainly of finely milled peat moss and vermiculite. The Territorial Seed Company recommends a simple 50/50 mix of vermiculite and peat moss,[37] but some authorities recommend adding compost to the mix because it can suppress diseases.[38] Some farmers also add a little clean sand. If these latter two ingredients are added, they shouldn't constitute more than 1/3 of the soil volume in aggregate.

Don't use garden soil, and don't use potting soil. It is extremely important that any compost used to make seed-starting mix be well finished so that it contains no disease organisms or weed seeds. (Garden soil can be used as an ingredient if it is first sifted through a 1/4-inch mesh screen and then sterilized. Instructions for sterilizing are given later in this chapter. Potting soil can be used under the same conditions—if it is sifted then sterilized.) A little compost or worm castings mixed into seed-starting mixes is fine and can be helpful in warding off diseases.

But even organic fertilizer in too great a concentration will create an environment ideal for the growth of various fungi that will invade and harm the seedlings. An indoor seed-starting environment is not like the great outdoors. Wind movement, sunshine, and other elements that keepfungi at bay are greatly reduced in an indoor environment. As a result, the teaspoon of solid fertilizer that does so much good outdoors can be harmful to seedlings.

Another reason for keeping the nutrient content of seed-starting medium low is the lower nutrient concentrations cause more aggressive root growth. Improved root growth leads to a transplant that will suffer less shock when it is planted outdoors.

Here is my own recipe: Finely milled sphagnum peat moss, 4 quarts Medium vermiculite, 1 pint Well-finished compost passed through a 1/4-inch screen made from hardware cloth, 1 pint Worm castings (available at any agricultural store), 1 pint Again, the simple 50/50 mix of peat moss and vermiculite recommended by the Territorial Seed Company and most commercial seed-starting mixes work perfectly fine. Feel free to experiment! Because the starting medium used for seeds is deliberately nutritionally poor and provided in insufficient quantity to meet a seedling's nutritional needs, it will become necessary to fertilize seedlings periodically once their first "true" leaves appear. The first two leaves that appear, called the cotyledons, contain a storehouse of nutrients that will keep the plant well supplied until the first true leaves emerge. (Plants can be divided into two categories—those with two cotyledons, called "dicots," and those with one cotyledon, called "monocots." The first true leaves look like the leaves that are distinctive for that plant.) Adding solid fertilizer to the cells of a seedling tray would be both harmful and impractical, so liquid fertilizer will need to be used. Seedlings are delicate, and full-strength fertilizer is both unneeded and potentially harmful. A good organic kelp, fish, or start-up fertilizer diluted to half strength and applied every two weeks after the first true leaves appear should work fine.

Containers

Mini-farming is not a small hobby operation. The average minifarmer will grow hundreds or perhaps thousands of seedlings. The best methods for starting seeds on this scale include cellular containers like those used by nurseries, peat pellets, and compressed soil blocks. The use of undivided flats is advocated in the Grow Biointensive method. In this method, a rectangular wooden box of convenient size and about 2 inches deep is filled with starting medium, and seeds are planted at close intervals.

The seeds are kept moist and warm, and once the cotyledons have appeared, the seedlings are carefully picked out and transplanted into a new flat with a greater distance between seedlings. This process is repeated again when the growth of the plant makes it necessary, and the final time the plant is transplanted, complete with a block of soil, it goes straight into the garden. The most obvious benefit of this method is that it is inexpensive. The largest detriment is that it is extremely timeconsuming.

Grow Biointensive publications also state that this method produces a beneficial microclimate and stronger transplants, but my own experiments have shown no appreciable difference between seedlings grown this way and seedlings grown exclusively in soil blocks or peat pellets. Certainly, this technique works well, and in a situation where the farmer is rich in time but poor in cash, it is a very good option. The commercial growers who make the small six-packs of transplants for the garden center use plastic multicelled containers. These containers cost money, of course, but also save on labor costs and are easily transplanted.

These units have a hole in the bottom of every cell, fit into rectangular plastic boxes that providefor bottom watering, and can be picked up at most agricultural stores for around $2 or $3 for a tray and eight 6-pack containers. The price of these works out to about $6 per 100 plants, which isn't expensive considering that the containers can be reused year to year as long as they are well washed between uses so they don't spread diseases. If you sell seedlings, as I do, you will want to take the cost of these containers (and labels) into account in setting your price. In practice, once acquired, the economics of using these is sound since the per-plant cost drops dramatically after the first year, and they save a lot of time compared to using undivided flats.

Broccoli seedlings destined for market. The disadvantage of multicelled containers is that each cell contains only two or three cubic inches of soil. This means that the soil can't hold enough nutrients to see the seedling through to transplanting time, so bottom watering with liquid fertilizer is required. Also, because of the small amount of space, roots grow to the sides of the cell and then wind around and around, contributing to transplant shock. Finally, because of the small soil volume, multicelled containers can't be left unattended for more than a couple of days because their water supply is depleted rapidly. Even with these disadvantages, they are the method of choice for producing seedlings for sale because of their convenience. Peat pellets have a significant advantage over multicelled containers when it comes to transplant shock.

Taking a transplant from a multicelled pack and putting it directly into garden soil canset the plant back for a few days as it acclimates to the new soil conditions. Peat pellets get around this problem because transplants are put into the garden without being disturbed, and roots can grow right through them into the soil. This allows for gradual acclimatization and virtually eliminates transplant shock. Peat pellets cost about $5 per 100 and can be purchased at agricultural supply stores and occasionally at places like Walmart.

They come as compressed dry wafers and are expanded by placing them in warm water. Once the pellets expand, the seeds are placed in the center and lightly covered, then the pellet is bottom watered as needed until time to plant in the garden. In the case of peat pellets, the seed-starting mix of a peat pellet is essentially devoid of nutrients altogether, making liquid fertilizer a must. If you use peat pellets, be sure to carefully slit and remove the webbing at transplanting time so it doesn't bind the roots.

Peat pots suffer from the same disadvantages that affect multicelled containers because of their small soil volume, plus they don't break down well, and they constrain root growth in many cases, so I don't recommend them. When I worked some compost into my beds last spring, I dug up perfectly intact peat pots that had been planted a year earlier.

Peat pots often fail to break down quickly.

Compressed soil blocks, while not aesthetically acceptable for commercial sale, are the best available choice for the farmer's own seedlings. That's because a compressed soil block contains 400% more soil volume than a peat pellet or multicelled container, meaning it will contain more nutrients and moisture. Seedlings raised in compressed soil blocks using a properly constituted soil mix may require no liquid fertilizer at all. Because roots grow right up to the edge of the block instead of twisting around, and the block is made of soil so decomposition isn't an issue, transplant shock all but disappears.

They are also the least expensive option when used in volume. Compressed soil blocks are made with a device called a "soil blocker" into which a soil mix is poured, and the mix is then compressed. A standard mix for the soil used in the blocker contains 30% fine peat moss, 30% good finished compost, 30% sterilized garden soil and 10% fine sand.39 A balanced organic fertilizer such as Cockadoodle DOO is added to the mix at the rate of 1/2 cup per four gallons of soil mix, and the pH is adjusted with lime if necessary to fall between 6.2 and 7.0. My own mix is 50% peat moss, 40% worm castings, and 10% coarse vermiculite with a bit of balanced fertilizer. (Garden soil can be sterilized by spreading it no more than 1-inch thick on a baking pan and baking in the oven at 200 degrees for 20 minutes. Don't use a good pan!) It is important that the ingredients used in a soil mix be sifted so large twigs don't interfere with the operation of the soil blocker.

A standard 2-inch soil blocker with rectangular inserts. Even though the devices for making soil blocks cost about $30 each, they are made of steel and will last many years, so they will save many times their cost compared to multicelled containers. I bought mine from Peaceful Valley Farm Supply over the Internet. One particular technique for using soil blockers merits attention. An insert can be purchased for the 2-inch soil blocker that makes a 3/4-inch cubic indentation in the block to accept 3/4-inch soil blocks. This is a great idea because it allows germination to be accomplished in smaller soil blocks that are then transplanted into the larger ones. That way you aren't taking up a large soil block with seed that won't germinate.

Use 1/4-inch hardware cloth to screen out debris.

Soil blocks with sprouted lettuce seedlings.

Light

Plants evolved with needs for light intensity that match the output of the sun, which provides light that is so intense that merely looking at it can permanently damage the eye. Naturally, seedlings grown inside also need an intense light source that can provide enough light without also making so much heat that plants get burned. With the exception of certain flowers, most plants do not need light to germinate. In fact some plants, like those in the brassica family, may have their germination inhibited by light. But once the first plant parts emerge above the ground, all plants need light to grow. In most of North America and Europe, there is not enough sunshine coming through even a south-facing window to adequately start seedlings during the winter months when most seed starting takes place, so a source of artificial light is required. Selecting an artificial light source should be based on an understanding of the plants' requirements. Plants require light of various wavelengths or colors for various purposes. Red wavelengths, for example, regulate dormancy, seed production, and tuber formation, whereas blue wavelengths stimulate chlorophyll production and vegetative growth. Violet wavelengths affect plants' tendency to turn toward a light source. The best light sources for starting seedlings, then, should generate a wide spectrum of light wavelengths that encompass both the blue and the red ends of the spectrum. There is a growing number of options for artificial lighting; unfortunately, most of these are quite expensive. Following is my particular approach that inexpensively meets the light needs for seedlings.

A homemade rack for seedlings works great and costs little.

All sorts of special carts costing anywhere from $200 to $1,000 are sold for this purpose, but with a little ingenuity you can create a suitable contrivance, made like the one illustrated, at very low cost. This device is made from a simple wire rack sold in the hardware department of Walmart for $50. Three racks hold up to four large seed trays each, and two 48-inch shop light fluorescent light fixtures are hung over each rack using simple adjustable chains from the hardware store. This way, the lights can be independently raised and lowered to keep them the right distance above the plants as they grow. The six lights (or fewer if you don't need them all) are plugged into an electric outlet strip that is plugged into a timer. Each light holds two 40-watt 48-inch fluorescent tubes.

The fluorescent tubes need to be selected with the needs of plants in mind. Cool white fluorescents put out more blue light, and warm white fluorescents put out more red light. Combining the two in the same fixture gives a perfectly acceptable mix of wavelengths. It's what I use, and a good many farmers use it successfully. 40 There are also special tubes for fluorescent light fixtures that are specifically designed for growing plants or duplicating the sun's wavelengths—and these work well too but at a cost roughly six times higher than regular tubes and at a reduced light output.

The thing to watch for with fluorescent lighting generally is light output, because plants need a lot of it. Go with the highest light output tubes that will fit in a 48-inch shop light fixture. Because the lights are used approximately five months out of the year, the tubes need to be replaced only every other year. Replace them even if they look and work fine, because after being used for two years, their measurable light output will have declined.

The intensity of light decreases in inverse proportion to the square of the distance from the source. In other words, the further away the lights are, the less light the plants will get. Fluorescent tubes need to be set up so that they are only an inch or two above the seedlings for them to get enough light. Because plants grow, either the height of the lights or the bottom of the plants needs to be adjustable. Plants need a combination of both light and darkness to complete their metabolic processes, so too much of either can be a bad thing. Because even closely spaced florescent lights are an imperfect substitute for true sunshine, the lights should be put on an inexpensive timer so seedlings get 16 hours of light and 8 hours of darkness every day. Don't forget: Once seeds sprout, shine the light on them!

Temperature

Many publications provide various tables with all sorts of data about the optimum temperatures for germination of different garden seeds. For starting seeds in the house, almost all seeds normally used to start garden seedlings will germinate just fine at ordinary room temperatures. The only time temperature could become an issue is if the area used for seed starting regularly falls below 60 degrees or goes above 80. If seed-starting operations get banished to the basement or garage where temperatures are routinely below 60 degrees, germination could definitely become a problem. The easiest solution for this situation is to use a heat mat (available at any agricultural supply store) underneath your flats that will raise the soil temperature about 20 degrees higher than the surrounding air. A heating mat is especially useful for peppers and tomatoes.

Water

Seedlings should be bottom watered by placing their containers (which contain holes in the bottom or absorb water directly) in water and allowing the starting medium to evenly water itself by pulling up whatever water is needed. Seedlings are delicate and their roots are shallow, so top watering can disrupt and uncover the vulnerable roots. It is important that the starting medium be kept moist, but not soaking, for the entire germination period. Once the germination process has begun and before the seedling emerges, allowing the seed to dry out will kill it.

Most containers used for seedlings are too small to retain an appreciable amount of water; for this reason seedlings should stay uniformly damp (though not soggy) until transplanted. Unfortunately, dampness can cause problems with mold growth. Often, such mold is harmless, but sometimes it isn't, and telling the difference before damage is done is difficult. If gray fuzz or similar molds appear on top of the seedling container, cut back the water a bit, and place the container in direct sunlight in a south-facing window for a few hours a day for two or three days.

This should take care of such a problem. Another cause of mold is the use of domes over top of seedling flats. These domes are advertised to create an environment "just like a greenhouse." In reality, they create an environment extremely conducive to mold, even in moderately cool temperatures. No matter how clean and sterile the starting medium, anytime I have ever used a dome on top of a seed flat, mold has developed within two or three days. I recommend that you do not use domes.

Fertilizer

As mentioned earlier, once seedlings have their first set of true leaves, they should be bottom watered with a half-strength solution of organic liquid fertilizer once every two weeks in addition to regular watering. Since starting medium is nutritionally poor, some fertilizer will be a benefit to the seedlings, but anything too concentrated can hurt the delicate developing root system and cause problems with mold. The only exception to this is soil blocks, which can contain enough nutrients that liquid fertilizer isn't needed because of their greater soil volume.

Hardening Off

A week or two before the intended transplant date, you may wish to start the process of "hardening off" the transplants; that is, the process of gradually acclimating the plants to the outdoor environment. This generally means bringing the seedlings outside and exposing them to sun and wind for an hour the first day, progressing to all day on the last day of the hardening-off period, which lasts about a week before transplanting. The process of hardening off serves to make the transplants more hardy. In my experience, hardening off makes little difference with plants that are transplanted after the last frost, but it does have an effect on the hardiness of plants that are transplanted before the last frost.

It should be done with all transplants anyway, because there is no way to know with absolute certainty if an unusual weather event will occur. I've seen no case in which hardening off transplants has been harmful and numerous cases in which it has helped so it is a good general policy for a mini-farm in which maximum yields are important.

Chapter Three
Season extensionin Mini-Farming

While season extension isn't an absolute necessity for the mini-farmer, it has some advantages. The most obvious is that season extension will allow you to grow warm season crops like sweet potatoes that require more growing days than available in your area, but there are other less obvious advantages. A simple, unheated hoop house, constructed with two layers of plastic, will allow many crops, such as parsnips and carrots, to be stored in the ground rather than harvested in fall. It will also allow many biennial plants, such as cabbage, to successfully overwinter for purposes of seed production.

Finally, it will allow you to grow many cold-hardy crops for sale or consumption, such as spinach and other salad greens. Along with these more practical benefits comes the psychological value (for us northeastern farmers) that such a structure will have in midwinter when the inviting growing foliage can be seen inside against a backdrop of dismal snow. There are a lot of approaches to season extension ranging from simple cold frames to fancy heated greenhouses with specialized glass and framing. The approach to this, as with everything else in mini-farming, is economic. Cold frames are simple, four-sided rectangles that are open on the bottom and sloped on the top and oriented so that the downward end of the slope faces the sun. Usually, they are covered with old windows, so they can be made cheaply. The only heat provided is that of the sun, so they can be placed just about anywhere. A cold frame will provide a temperature about 20 degrees warmer than the outside air during the day but will drop to within 5 degrees of outside temperature overnight unless it is well insulated or has provisions for heat retention.

If raised beds are used, cold frames can easily be made to fit. Hotbeds are cold frames that have a mechanism for heating built in. A couple of hundred years ago, hotbeds were made by digging a pit three feet deep, filling it to within six inches of the top with fresh horse manure that would provide heat as it composted and then covering that with six inches of regular garden soil in which crops were planted. More modern hotbeds use either buried heating cables underneath where the plants grow or pipes carrying warm water. Obviously, hotbeds keep crops warmer than cold frames, but the amount of warmth they provide varies with design.

A cold frame can extend the season by several weeks.

The unheated hoop house is a simple skeleton framework of hoops covered with the kind of plastic that folks in the northern parts of the United States use to cover their windows during the winter. Because it holds a far greater volume of air, it will tend to provide more warmth than a cold frame.

For farmers who are handy, there are also a number of free plans available on the Internet, including an easily built and inexpensive structure designed by Travis Saling viewable at westsidegardener.com. The pvcplans .com Web site has a number of free plans available describing how to make greenhouses from PVC pipe. The idea of an unheated environment that gets all of its heat from the sun can be taken further to create a solar greenhouse. Unlike a hoop house, which is translucent on all sides, a solar greenhouse is translucent only on the side facing the sun, and the other sides are insulated to retain heat while drums of water painted black sit against the back wall creating a solar mass. Portions of the back wall are often reflective to put more light onto the plants.

A solar greenhouse is certainly more expensive to construct than a hoophouse, but it has the advantage of having smaller ongoing operational costs than a traditional greenhouse because it doesn't use supplemental heating. Either a hoop house or a solar greenhouse can be made into a heated greenhouse by adding supplemental heat. Supplemental heat can be provided by a heating appliance of practically any type compatible with your budget.

What to Grow

The decision on what to grow decides the design of the season extension adopted, rather than the other way around. Miner's lettuce grows only a couple of inches tall, so it will work fine in a cold frame, but kale is so tall that a hoop house would be required. Winter-hardy crops like spinach and kale don't require supplemental heat, lettuce would require only a little, and tender crops like tomatoes would require a considerable amount. Especially with increasing fuel costs, it is important to consider whether growing frost-tender crops like tomatoes in the winter makes economic sense, and most often it does not. I recommend growing hardy crops using no supplemental heat or semihardy crops using just enough supplemental heat to prevent freezing.

Under such conditions, growth of crops is slow, and it is best to establish them late in the summer or early in the fall so that by the time winter hits, the season extender is serving mainly to extend the harvest rather than actively grow crops. So what crops are suitable for this purpose? Carrots, parsnips, and parsley will do well in a hoop house or cold frame. Both parsnips and carrots started at midsummer will taste sweet come January. Salsify planted just at the first fall frost can be harvested abit past Yule.

Many leaf lettuces will grow, though their outer leaves may sustain some damage. (Try the Winter Density variety.) Beets will hold in the ground in a cold frame, and chard may grow if you are south of Pennsylvania. Kale will hold well and even grow, as will Brussels sprouts and green onions or leeks. (The American Flag variety of leek will work well.)

There are a few particularly cold-hardy crops ideal for season extension, including miner's lettuce, corn salad (a.k.a. "mache"), italian dandelion, wintercress, and purslane. While these are unusual, they are a real taste-treat that adds character to winter salads. Besides winter crops, an unheated hoop house can also help the farmer get a head start on spring season crops and even extend the season long enough to grow crops or varieties that would otherwise be impossible, such as the aforementioned sweet potatoes in the Northeast. A hoop house also expands the possibilities for cover crops and green manures because of the change in environment.

Special Considerations

A hoop house, cold frame, or hotbed is inherently protected from precipitation. The good news is water is completely in the farmer's control. The bad news is the lack of rainfall will tend to concentrate salts in the soil in the protected area, which will hurt plant growth. It takes three or four years for this to happen, but it is still a problem. Another problem with a more permanent structure is that the space within it can accumulate pests and diseases. Especially since pests have nowhere to go, the enclosed area can cancel someof the benefits of crop rotation within that space.

The most space-efficient way to handle this is to make the structure easily erected and dismantled, and dismantle it late every spring. For more permanent greenhouse designs, the plastic can be removed during the late spring through early fall, which would have the same effect. For large structures, such as 90-foot-long greenhouses, it is obviously too time-consuming, but for structures of the size usually employed in a mini-farm, it is will be feasible if they are designed with easy maintenance in mind. Larger farms in Europe and the United States have movable greenhouses on rails that are rolled from one location to another with each season to accommodate growing needs and diminish the problems of a permanent standing structure. This may be a bit beyond the needs of a mini-farmer, but it can be accomplished with a little ingenuity and moderate expense by a farmer who is so inclined.

Improving Greenhouse Efficiency

An unheated hoop house can do a great deal to extend the growing season, but a few simple modifications at very low cost can dramatically improve the light and heat utilization of such a structure. In the winter when the sun is low in the sky, a good proportion of the light that hits a hoop house will enter the south side and exit the north side without ever touching a plant. If a reflective sheet is installed along the entire north wall up to the ridge pole, light that would otherwise escape will get reflected back onto the plants, thus increasing the light available to the plants and raising the temperature. A good material for this purpose isreflective insulation, available inexpensively from most home improvement stores.

Not only will the aluminum surface of the insulation reflect light, but it will also reflect 97% of radiant heat that would have escaped through the plastic back into the hoop house. The next modification is to add a method of heat retention. A simple hoop house will lose temperature quickly after sunset, and one way to slow down the temperature drop is to line up a number of black-painted barrels against the north wall of the hoop house—though not actually touching the reflective insulation—and fill them with water. The drums of water will absorb the heat from the sunlight during the day and then radiate that heat back into the hoop house at night.

The value of this approach is enhanced by the addition of the reflective insulation because the radiant heat gets reflected back into the enclosed space from all directions. Barrels can be emptied and moved anytime the greenhouse is moved, or they can be used for raising fish, with exchanged water being used as nitrogen-rich liquid fertilizer. (Yes, fish can be raised in a barrel using the technology of aquaculture, but aquaculture isn't covered in this book.) So, what happens if there is no sun for a week and the water drums freeze? South of Connecticut, this is unlikely to be a problem, but it is a possibility further north. You may need to abandon using barrels or abandon the simple hoop house design altogether and build a solar greenhouse. There are a number of solar greenhouse designs available on the Internet. What they all have in common is significant insulation (R-30) everywhere but in the windows that face south and reflective coating on all interior walls.

Portable Hoops for Raised Beds

Raised beds lend themselves to easily constructed and inexpensive attachments for season extension, particularly if constructed with a width of four feet. The easiest attachments are cold frames mentioned earlier and portable hoops.

Loops on the frame of a raised bed. Raised beds can be equipped to accept portable hoops by attaching 1-inch rings to the outside of the beds at the ends and every two feet. The portable hoops are made from 10-foot-long pieces of 1/2inch PVC pipe that have been cut in half for ease of storage. To build the hoops, the two 5-foot pieces of PVC are connected via a straight coupling, and then each end is inserted into one of the 1inch rings on each side of the bed. The hoops are covered with translucent plastic sheeting 10 feet wide available at any hardware store. The plastic can be secured at the long edges by sandwiching it between 1-inch × 2-inch boards so it can be easily rolled up and deployed, or it can by secured with homemade snap clips made by slicing pieces of garden hose lengthwise. Which technique will work best depends on the strength of prevailing winds in your area. Insert the PVC pipes into the loops.

Completed hoop house.

Chapter Four
Fruit: trees and vines

Fruit trees and vines can provide an enormous amount of foodcompared to the effort invested. Many fruit and nut trees produce, literally, bushels of fruits or nuts, and some blackberry variants produce gallons of berries per vine. Unfortunately, even though berries may even produce in their first or second season, full-sized fruit and nut trees take several years to come into production and may produce nothing at all for the first few years. Dwarf trees will normally produce fruit within three years, but the volume of fruit they produce is lower.

To offset this problem, diversify! If possible, in the year preceding the start of your mini-farm, plant a small section with berry and perhaps some grape vines for the next year's harvest. Along with these, plant dwarf fruit trees and some full-sized nut trees. In this way, the harvest starts modestly with berries the first year and expands to include dwarf cherries the next year, dwarf apples the year after that, and so on. Within seven years, the farmer is producing enough fruit and nuts for the family plus some surplus.

Fruits are full of idiosyncrasies in terms of disease and pest problems, pruning requirements, suitable climate, and so on. This is particularly true of vinifera grapes, apples, peaches, and other popular fruits. In addition to ordering high-quality trees

that are likely to be less susceptible to problems, you should
work proactively to keep pest problems minimal by making sure
plants that attract beneficial insects are already established
where the trees will be planted. Mostnotably, this means clover.
Clover attracts insects that feast on the most tenacious pests of
apple-family trees and fruits such as codling moths, apple
maggots, and plum curculios. The exact type of clover to be
planted will vary with the condition of the soil, expected
temperatures, and expected precipitation.

A good resource for selecting the right variety of clover is a
comprehensive organic gardening catalog like that from
Peaceful Valley Farm Supply. Plant trees in the spring, and spray
them for the first time in the fall with dormant oil that smothers
and controls overwintering insects. The following spring spray
the trees with a lighter horticultural oil in spring when the buds
have swelled but not yet blossomed. Also spray them with either
a lime sulfur or organic copper-based fungicide according to
label directions every spring after their first year.

Traps for common problem insects such as codling moths or
apple maggots should be set out and maintained at a high
enough density to trap out all of the males of the species. Fruits
and nuts often have specific pollination requirements that make
it necessary to plant more than one tree. Sometimes the trees
have to be of slightly different variants because trees of the same

variety were propagated by grafting and are therefore genetically identical and self-sterile.

A few nurseries sell trees propagated from seed rather than grafting, and these trees will pollinate each other without issue even if the same variety. Be sure to pay attention to catalog information and ask questions of the nursery staff to avoid later disappointment! Pruning will be necessary to maximize the productive potential of the trees. There are many schools of thought on the subject of pruning, and numerous weighty tomes have been written, but the basics are easily described.

Blackberries and Raspberries

Cane fruits, like raspberries and blackberries, grow long and heavy enough that the tips of the canes touch the ground—where they then set a new root and grow more new canes. This isn't necessarily desirable, as it leads to an ever-expanding impenetrable thorny mess, so it is best to trellis the canes to prevent this. The easiest trellising for cane fruits is a four-foot-tall "T" at each end of the row of canes with galvanized wire run from each end of the T along the length of the row. The wire holds up the canes so they don't touch the ground, and new canes are trained to stay behind the wire. This makes the berries easy to pick as well.

Raspberries are nutritious and easy to grow. Blackberries are pruned by distinguishing between primocanes and floricanes. Primocanes are canes in their first year that bear leaves but no flowers or fruit. Floricanes are those same canes in their second year, when they bear flowers and fruit. After a cane has fruited, it slowly dies, so fruiting canes should be cut out and removed once their fruiting season has passed. Primocanes should b e topped during their first year of growth, meaning they should have their tops cut off just about 4 inches above the trellis. This will cause them to send out lateral shoots so that when they bear fruit the next year, they will bear more abundantly. 43 The lateral shoots should be trimmed to 12 inches to 18 inches.

This sort of T-trellis is easily made and works well

The same general technique applies to raspberries, with some minor changes. Yellow and red raspberries shouldn't be topped, and the laterals that form on purple and black raspberries should be trimmed to just 10 inches. Ever-bearing raspberry varieties fruit in the late summer of the primocane stage and then again in the early summer of the floricane stage. After the early summer fruiting, the floricanes should be removed. The easiest way to distinguish floricanes in ever-bearing raspberries is that the first-year fruit is on the top of the cane and the second-year fruit is at the bottom.44

Grapes

Grapes can be divided into three general varieties: European, American, and muscadine. European grape varieties (Vitisvinifera) are vulnerable to a nasty pest called phylloxera, which is a tiny louselike insect that causes all sorts of problems, especially in the eastern United States. Muscadine grapes, native to the southern United States, can be successfully grown only south of Maryland because of their climate requirements. Other American grape varieties are naturally resistant to phylloxera and can be grown practically anywhere in the continental United States. For varietal wine production, scion wood of European grape varieties is often grafted onto American variety root stocks to reduce their vulnerability to phylloxera.

Since grape vines are expensive and can last for decades, it is important to pick a grape variety appropriate for your local climate. Check a reputable vendor for recommendations. All grape varieties can be used to produce jams, jellies, raisins, and wines for home use. Grapes do best in moderately fertile soil because soil as fertile as that in a vegetable garden will cause the leaves to grow so quickly and in such volume that the fruit will be shaded by the leaves, which will keep them damp and increase the likelihood of disease.

Properly pruned grape vines yield good crops.

It is possible to start a grape vine in the fall, but odds of success are far greater if it is started in the spring because that gives the transplant more time to get established and store energy in its root system for overwintering. When you first bring home a grape vine, it will likely have numerous shoots coming out of the root system. Cut off all of the shoots but the strongest one, then cut that one back to only three or four buds. Plant the vine in well-drained soil in a locale with plenty of sun, and water thoroughly. Pretty soon new shoots will emerge at the buds, plus some more from the roots. Cut off the ones that emerge from the roots, and once the new shoots from the buds have grown to about 12 inches, select the best and strongest of these and cut off the others.

The best shoot will be pretty much upright. Drive a strong stake into the ground close to the plant, and throughout the summer keep the shoot tied nice and straight to that stake. Meanwhile, set up your training and trellising system. There are many types, but about the easiest is the Kniffin system using two horizontal galvanized steel wires at three feet and six feet from the ground tied to two strong posts secured in the ground. The first spring a year after planting, take the chosen shoot (which should have grown to a length somewhat taller than the bottom wire), and select the two strongest lateral shoots and tie those to the bottom wire while continuing to tie the growing trunk vertically to the stake.

Later in the season, once the growing trunk has grown to slightly below or slightly above the top wire, cut it off there and select the two strongest lateral shoots to tie to the top horizontal wires. Occasionally, the chosen shoot that will serve as the trunk won't put out lateral shoots the first year. If that occurs—it's no big deal. Grape vines are vigorous and forgiving, so if a mistake is made in one year, it can always be corrected the next year. Just take the main shoot that serves as the trunk once it is slightly above the first wire, and tie it to one side of the wire and trim it back to three or four buds. These will form shoots. Select the two strongest of these —one of which will be run horizontally in the opposite direction on the wire, and the other of which will be run vertically up the stake and handled as detailed previously. Ongoing pruning will be important to maintain fruit production because grapes produce on the shoots that come from one-year-old wood. So any shoots that arise from wood that is more than one year old won't bear fruit. That means that the horizontal shoots selected the first year should be removed for the second year andnew shoots from the trunk trained along the wires.

The Kniffin system is one of the easiest for training grapes.

The foregoing is not the final word on grape pruning and

training, as many other systems are available to those desiring more information—but this should be enough to get you started. Grapes are prone to black rot and botrytis fungus, as well as birds and deer. Because of the rot and fungal problems, it is important to avoid sprinkler irrigation of grapes and practice good sanitation by consistently removing old fruit and leaves at the end of each season. A copper-based fungicide applied at bloom time is most effective against rot and fungus.45 On a small scale, birds and deer can be foiled with netting; on a larger scale, some creativity (such as noisemakers and fencing) will be required. I grow my grapes far away from everything else, and the birds and deer haven't found them so far!

Strawberries

Very few fruits are as prolific and easy to grow in limited space as

strawberries. Moreover, because of their delicate nature, they are expensive to ship long distances, so they sell well in season if you decide to market them. Beds are easy to establish and require minimal maintenance on the scale of a mini-farm. Strawberries come in three basic types: spring-bearing, everbearing, and day-neutral. The spring-bearing variety produces a single crop; the ever-bearing variety produces crops in spring, summer, and fall; and the day-neutral strawberry produces fruit throughout the season. Spring-bearing varieties can be early season, middle season, or late season, meaning that through careful selection of more than one spring-bearing variety, it is possible to extend the length of harvest substantially. Consider the intended use of the strawberries—preservation or fresh eating—in selecting varieties for either a continuous small crop or one or more larger harvests.

Strawberries do extremely well in raised beds. Strawberry plants can be spread either through seeds or through plants and runners. The best bet in most cases is to buy strawberry plants of known characteristics and then let them spread by runners. Runners are a long stem that emerges from the crown of the strawberry plant and establishes a new crown and root system wherever it contacts suitable earth. Simply place the runners where they will fill in the gaps in your planting—no more than four strawberry plants per square foot.

Strawberries should be well fertilized with compost and any needed organic amendments and be mulched with straw or fallen leaves after the last frost. They occasionally fall prey to botyritis blight, a gray mold that can grow on the berries. To keep this controlled, keep the beds clear of debris, make sure strawberries are harvested when ripe or slightly underripe, and spray with an organic fixed-copper fungicide as needed.

Apples and Pears

Apples and pears are the quintessential home fruit trees and can be grown in almost any part of the United States. A wide selection of modern and heirloom varieties are available that are suitable for fresh eating, preservation, and pies. Apples and pears offered in nurseries are usually produced by grafting the scion wood of the desired variety onto a more hardy compatible rootstock, such as that of flowering crab. The original rootstock can produce shoots below the graft (known as "suckers"), and these should be trimmed as soon as they are spotted. Apples and pears should be pruned and trained when they are quite young or else they will become difficult to manage and produce inferior fruit. The objective of training the tree is to provide optimal air circulation and sunlight while keeping the fruit low enough to the ground so that it can be picked without a crane.

Pears are a bit easier than apples to keep pest free.

It is easiest for a mini-farmer is to select dwarf or semidwarf trees from the beginning. This will reduce pruning requirements and make maintenance easier and safer. Ideally, the tree will be pruned so that the shape is similar to a Christmas tree, which will allow maximum penetration of sunlight and easiest spraying while keeping the greatest bulk of the fruit closest to the ground. A large number of articles on the specifics of pruning and training pomme fruits are available, but it isn't hard to master if a few rules are followed. (Apples, pears, and quinces are collectively referred to as pomme fruits. The word pomme comes from the French word for apple.)

When the young tree is first planted, tie it to a straight, eight-footlong stake driven at least three feet into the soil for strength, cut off any limbs that are larger than 50% of the diameter of the trunk, and trim the trunk back to a height of three feet. Branches are strongest when they leave the trunk at an angle between 60 and 75 degrees, so when the branches are young, it is easy to bring them back to that angle by tying them with string or inserting small pieces of wood between the branch and the trunk. The branches on trees will tend to grow toward the sun, so that tendency will have to be countered the same way because you want the tree to grow straight and well balanced. Subsequent pruning is best done in late winter or very early spring.

The first spring after planting, remove any limbs closer to the ground than two feet and any limbs that are larger than 50% of the diameter of the trunk. If the tree has developed more than seven limbs, select the seven best distributed around the tree to be saved, and prune the rest. It is important when a limb is pruned that it be pruned back all the way to the trunk, otherwise it will sprout a bunch of vertically growing wood and create troubles. Once the pruning is done, limbs that need it should be tied or fitted with spacers to get the right angle to the trunk.

Beware of cutting off just the tips of the remaining limbs, because this can delay fruiting. Once the tree has been fruiting for a couple of years, such cuts can be used sparingly for shaping, but it is better to solve shading problems by removing entire limbs. For all following years use the same rules by aiming for a wellbalanced upright tree without excessive shading.

Stone Fruits

Stone fruits include cherries, apricots, peaches, plums, and nectarines. Because most stone fruits are native to warm climates and are thus susceptible to problems from winter injury or frost killing the flowers in the spring, it is important to carefully select varieties suitable for your area by consulting with a knowledgeable seller with a good reputation. No matter what cultivar is selected, it should be planted in an area protected from wind and with good sunshine and drainage. It is best to select a one-year-old tree five or six feet tall with good root growth. Like apples and pears, stone fruits can be grafted onto dwarfing rootstocks. Unfortunately, none of the dwarf varieties grow well north of Pennsylvania.46 The good news is that a number of hardy stone fruit varieties native to North America are available. The bush cherry (Prunus

Nectarines are easy to grow and easy to can or freeze. besseyi),
American wild plum (Prunusamericana), and American beach
plum (Prunusmaritima) can be grownthroughout the
continental United States, and Indian blood peach
(Prunuspersica) can be grown south of Massachusetts. All of
these are available in seed form from Bountiful Gardens
(www.bountifulgardens.org) and are also available from a
number of nurseries. Almost all nursery stock is grafted rather
than grown from seed for a number of reasons, but the effect of
this is that if two trees of the same type and variety are selected,
they may be genetically the same exact plant and thus incapable
of pollinating each other, causing low fruit yields.

More than one of any stone fruit should be selected to aid in
pollination, and it is important to consult with knowledgeable
nursery personnel about exactly what varieties need to be grown
to ensure proper pollination. Space nectarines, peaches, plums,
and apricots anywhere from 15 to 20 feet apart, and space
cherries anywhere from 20 to 30 feet apart for best pollination
and fruit yields. Stone fruits should be planted in early spring by
digging a hole big enough to accommodate the entire root
system without bunching it up or looping it around and deep
enough that the graft union is about two inches above the

ground. Once the soil is filled back into the hole, the area should be watered thoroughly to help the soil settle around the roots.

Stone fruits should be fertilized in early spring only (using a balanced organic fertilizer) and never later in the summer. Fertilizing in late summer will cause vigorous growth that the root system hasn't grown enough to support so the tree could be harmed and have difficulty overwintering. By fertilizing in the early spring, the tree has a chance to grow in a balanced way across the entire growing season so it will overwinter properly.

A good fertilizer can be made by mixing together 1 pound of bone meal, 1/2 pound of dried blood, and 3 pounds of dried kelp or greensand. Apply 1/2 pound to the soil surface around the drip line of the tree (the "drip line" is the area on the ground just under the widest branches) by using a crowbar to make four to eight holes six inches deep in a circle around the plant and sprinkling some of the fertilizer in each hole. Use 1/2 pound the first year, then an additional half pound every year thereafter until, in the ninth and subsequent years, 5 pounds are being used each spring.

Stone fruits prefer a pH of 6.0 to 6.5, and if a soil test shows amendment to be needed, that can be done in the spring as well. Keep in mind, however, that lime can take several months to work, so don't overlime and raise the pH above 6.5. The following pruning directions are equally applicable to both dwarf and full-size trees. Because all stone fruits are susceptible to brown rot, they should be trained to an open center rather than a central leader (a single main trunk that reaches all the way to the top of the tree) like an apple tree. This will allow maximum light and air penetration to keep brown rot problems under control. When the tree is first planted, cut off any branches closer than 18 inches to the ground, and cut the central leader at 30 inches above the ground. This will force branches to grow out at 18 to 30 inches above the ground, which will yield branches at the right height when the tree is mature. Select three or four good branches that are growing evenly spaced around the trunk, and prune back the others all the way to the trunk, then prune back the central leader to just above the topmost selected branch. These selected branches will be the main scaffolds of the tree, referring to their structural importance. Stone fruit branches are strongest when they leave the trunk at an angle between 60 and 90 degrees, so now is the time to establish those angles and the direction of growth using a combination of ropes and wooden spacers inserted between the branch and the trunk.

Stone fruits should not be pruned in winter because of susceptibility to winter injury and because of a disease called cytospora canker. Rather, they should be pruned between the time they bloom and the first week after the flower petals have fallen. The first pruning after planting should occur just after blooming in the early spring of the next year. At that time, any branches that are broken and diseased should be removed, and the main scaffolds should be cut back half their length to an outward facing bud. Any vertically growing shoots should likewise be removed, and spacers or ties for maintaining branch angles should be checked and adjusted as necessary. The second pruning after planting will occur at the same time the next year. By this time, the main scaffold branches will be developing new branches on them. Select three or four sublimbs on each main scaffold to be preserved.

These should be on opposite sides of the scaffolds, not growing straight up or bending down, and be at least 18 inches away from the main trunk. The main scaffold branches should then be cut back by 1/3 to an outwardfacing bud, and all limbs but the selected sublimbs should be cut back to the branch or to the trunk as appropriate. Subsequent pruning simply needs to maintain the open center by removing vertical limbs and limbs that grow inward toward the center. Limbs and sublimbs should be headed back to an outwardfacing bud each year to make sure new fruiting wood is growing each year, and limbs should be pruned as needed to maintain the desired shape and size of tree and to avoid broken limbs.

Nut Trees

Compared to fruit trees, nut trees are easier to prune and care for. The only downside is that, except for filberts, they grow to be quite large and thus require as much as 50 feet between trees. Walnuts and, to a lesser extent, pecans and hickories produce a chemical called juglone in their root systems that inhibits the germination of other plants, so they shouldn't be planted close to a garden. A number of trees are unaffected by juglone, including cherries, oaks, pears, and most cone-bearing trees, among others. The only vegetables unaffected by juglone are onions, beans, carrots, corn, melons, and squash. Most nut trees aren't self-fruitful and therefore must be planted in pairs. The same caveat applies to nuts as to fruits in that many nut trees are made by grafting and thus are genetic clones. For this reason, two different varieties of the same nut will need to be planted unless those trees were grown from seed, in which case two trees of the same variety will work fine.

Chestnuts, walnuts, and other nuts are highly nutritious. Nut trees can be grown from seed as long as the requisite period of cold stratification is met to break dormancy. (Cold stratification means exposing the seed to a period of subfreezing temperature for a period of time. Many seeds for trees require this or they will never sprout.) If you plant the seed in the fall and protect it from rodents, it will sprout in the spring. Plant it about two feet deep and mulch with hay over the winter, then remove the mulch in early spring. The tree should be transplanted into a hole big enough to handle the entire root system.

About 2/3 of the soil should be carefully shoveled around the roots and then well watered and the remaining soil shoveled in and tamped down. The area around the tree should then be mulched to reduce competition with weeds and the trunk protected with a circular hardware cloth protector to keep deer and other critters from eating the bark. (Hardware cloth is available at any hardware store at minimal cost.)

Because nut trees have a long taproot that grows slowly, they need to have about half of their top growth pruned back during transplanting, leaving several buds. This balances the upper and lower portion of the tree to enhance survivability. New verticalgrowing shoots should emerge from the buds left behind, and when they are 8 to 12 inches long, the most vigorous should be selected as the tree's new central leader, and the remainder cut off even with the trunk. From that point forward, you are mainly aiming for a balanced tree, so prune to keep the tree balanced.

Conduct all pruning in late winter or very early spring, and remove all dead or damaged branches. At the same time, progressively shorten the lowest limbs a little each year until the tree is about 20 feet high, at which point all limbs lower than 6 feet should be removed flush with the trunk. This preserves the food-making ability of the lower limbs until it is no longer needed. Growing distance/productivity for such large trees can be troublesome on a small lot, but there are ways to get around the problem. Table 17 gives the ultimate distance that the trees should be from each other when fully grown.

Keep in mind that nut trees produce nuts long before reaching full

size and that nut wood is some of the most expensive, so selling it could net a nice bundle. If you wish to do so, plant the nut trees about 10 feet apart and then selectively harvest them for wood as their branches come close to touching. In the end, you have properly spaced highly productive nut trees and hopefully a wad of cash.

Chapter Five

Raising chicken for egg

If, for personal, health, or religious reasons you are opposed to consuming animal food products, then skip this chapter and the next one. If you are a meat eater but are understandably squeamish about eating homegrown eggs or turning animals into meat, I nevertheless encourage you to continue reading simply for your own knowledge. Nothing says "farm" like the sound of a rooster crowing in the morning, and nothing is more aggravating to neighbors than a rooster that seems to crow all day, every day. Still, small livestock have a place on the mini-farm because of the high-quality protein that they provide.

If you currently purchase meat and eggs, know that homegrown meat and eggs can be raised at a very low cost that will save you money. For the purposes of a mini-farm occupying half an acre or less, cows, goats, and similar livestock will place too high a demand on the natural resources of such a small space and will end up costing more than the value of the food they provide. In such small spaces, the greatest practical benefit can be derived from chickens, guineas, some species of ducks, and aquaculture. Rabbits are also a possibility, but remember that children (and adults!) can get attached to them easily. But chickens, overall, are the most costeffective choice on a small lot.

These chickens are so friendly they eat out of your hand.

Chickens are foragers that will eat grass, weeds, insects, acorns, and many other things they happen to run across. They will virtually eliminate grasshoppers, slugs, and other pests in the yard, thus keeping them away from the garden. Many cover crops like alfalfa, vetch, and soybeans are delicacies for birds and since cover crops are recommended to be grown anyway, a small flock of 10 or 20 birds can be raised with minimal feed expenditures over the growing season. Don't expect to get rich in the chicken and egg business because you would be competing at the wholesale level in a commodity market, so it's unlikely to be a direct money maker. But it is feasible to produce meat and eggs for yourself at costs that significantly undercut those of the supermarket while selling the odd dozen to friends and coworkers. On our own farm, the eggs we sell completely liquidate the cost of feed so that our own eggs are free, plus we get to keep the chickens valuable nitrogen-rich manure for our compost pile.

Chickens

A flock of 12 laying chickens costs about $6.00 per week to feed during the winter months when they can't be fed by foraging. They will earn their keep by producing about two to four dozen eggs weekly (more during the summer, fewer during the winter). Obviously, the family can't eat that many eggs, so a little negotiation with friends or coworkers who appreciate farm-fresh eggs will net you $2 to $3 per dozen. (Egg cartons cost about $0.20 each from a number of manufacturers. For more information, just type "egg cartons" into an Internet search engine. We get ours at a local gettogether known as a "chicken swap.") To put the cost of chicken feed into perspective, a flock of 12 chickens costs less to feed than a house cat.

At the supermarket, a chicken is just a chicken, but eggs run the gamut from cheap generic eggs costing less than a dollar a dozen to organic eggs costing more than five dollars a carton. From the standpoint of raising chickens, there are numerous breeds available, each of which has its strengths and weaknesses. Many chickens are bred specifically for meat yield, and others are bred mainly for laying eggs. There are also dual-purpose varieties that split the difference. For a mini-farm, I would recommend a hardy egg-laying variety such as the Rhode Island Red, which has the benefit of being good at hatching its own eggs over the more cultured Leghorn (pronounced "legern") varieties.

Another good choice would be a dual-purpose breed like the New Hampshire or Orpington. In my experience, the laying productivity of hens diminishes over time, so these birds can be transitioned into the freezer and replaced with younger hens. (Old layers transitioned into the freezer are tough and best used for soups, stews, and chicken pot pies, so label them accordingly.) If you choose to hatch eggs from your chickens to supplement your flock, new roosters of the chosen breed should be brought in every couple of years to reduce inbreeding. You'll find that hens and roosters are fun to watch and provide endless amusement.

When the farmer steps outside, plate in hand, to deliver meal leftovers to the chickens, they'll come running! Then, the chicken that managed to retrieve an especially attractive piece of food will be chased all over the place by other members of the flock.

The roosters will be vigilant and defend the rest of the flock against attack but otherwise just strut around looking proud and important. Chickens definitely establish a "pecking order" amongst themselves, so new chickens should be separated from the rest of the flock until they are large enough to defend themselves. You need only one rooster for every 20 or fewer hens. In fact, you need no roosters at all unless you are planning for the hens to raise babies. Too many roosters is a bad idea since they are equipped with spurs on their legs and will fight each other unless the flock is large enough to accommodate the number of roosters. Roosters are not usually dangerous to humans, but there have been cases of attacks against small children, so it's good to keep an eye on kids who are playing in the same yard with roosters. In addition, if your flock has fewer than 20 birds, the rooster will likely mount the chickens so often that they may develop bald spots.

With too few hens, roosters leave some bald spots.

Caring for Baby Chicks

All birds have requirements in common with any other livestock. They need special care during infancy, food, water, shelter, and protection from predators. Chickens can be started as eggs in a commercial or home-built incubator. Most often, they are purchased as day-old chicks. They can be obtained at the local feed and seed store in the spring or ordered from a reputable firm.

After hatching or arrival, baby birds should be provided with a brooder, food, and water. For a mini-farm-scaled operation, a brooder need be nothing more than an area enclosed on the sides free of drafts, an adjustable-height heat lamp, and a thermometer. (These products are available at agricultural supply stores.) The floor of the brooder should be smooth (like flat cardboard or newspapers) for the first few days until the chicks figure out how to eat from the feeder, and then you can add some wood shavings. Make sure to clean all the droppings and replace the litter daily.

Feeding and watering devices for baby birds are readily available. When the baby chicks are first introduced to the brooder, duck their beaks briefly in the water so they recognize it as a water source. Just before hatching, chicks suck up the last of the yolk so they are all set for up to 24 hours without food after hatching, but you want them to have food and water as soon as possible. Incubators and brooding areas must be thoroughly cleaned and disinfected before populating them in order to keep a disease called coccidiosis controlled. Coccidiosis is caused by a parasite that is spread through bird droppings and is more dangerous to baby birds than to adults. It is easy to tell if a baby bird has contracted the parasite because blood will appear in the droppings.

Feed for baby birds is often formulated with an additive for conferring immunity to the parasite; some small-scale poultry farmers report that the disease can be controlled by adding one tablespoon of cider vinegar per quart to the birds' drinking water for three days. Either way, the importance of cleanliness and disinfection in areas to be inhabited by baby birds can't be overemphasized.

Baby chicks in a brooder made from plywood.

Disinfection requires a thorough ordinary cleaning with soap and water to remove all organic matter followed by applying a suitable disinfectant for a sufficient period of time. A number of disinfectants are available including alcohols, phenolic compounds, quaternary ammonia disinfectants, and a large number of commercial products sold for that purpose. The most accessible suitable disinfectant is chlorine bleach diluted by adding 3/4 cup of bleach to one gallon of water. This requires a contact time of five minutes before being removed from the surface, then the area has to be well ventilated so it doesn't irritate the birds. Baby chicks should be started on a type of feed called "starter crumbles" and kept on it for six to eight weeks or until fully feathered. Once fully feathered, they can go on layer rations and be put in the hen house. They don't usually start laying eggs until they are a little over 16 weeks old.

Vaccinations

You should check with the agricultural extension agent in your local area for vaccination recommendations. Poultry are prone to certain diseases, such as Newcastle disease, that are easily protected against by vaccination but are incurable once contracted and can easily wipe out a flock. Most vaccines come in a size suitable for vaccinating 1,000 birds, which is not particularly suitable for a backyard flock.

I vaccinate my laying chickens for Newcastle disease and infectious bronchitis (IB). Newcastle disease is a highly contagious viral illness of birds that has been recognized since the 1920s. It manifests in various forms, some of which cause as much as 90% mortality in a flock. Newcastle disease infects and is spread by all manner of birds, and it is endemic throughout Western Europe and North America. Most birds don't experience the levels of mortality and debility that manifest in domestic chickens, though. It is primarily spread by droppings.

In plain English, this means that all that is needed for your flock to be wiped out is for a sparrow to poop into your chicken yard while flying over. (As a side note, the virus causes a mild conjunctivitis in humans and is particularly toxic to cancer cells in humans while leaving normal cells practically unharmed. Research into this is ongoing.) So vaccinating your flock is a good idea. Meanwhile, while the Newcastle vaccine is available on its own, it can also be purchased as a combined vaccine for IB. IB is caused by a highly contagious coronavirus that mutates rapidly.

While the immediate mortality rate from IB tends to be low, it can permanently damage the kidneys and reproductive tracts of chickens, hurts shell pigmentation, and makes the eggs unappetizing. Thus, especially if you visit the backyard flocks of other poultry owners, vaccinating your flock for IB makes sense. So, now that you've decided to vaccinate your flock, how do you go about doing it? First you have to get the vaccine—which I order from Jeffers Livestock. Trouble is, the teeny-weeny 7 ml (less than two teaspoons) vial contains enough dosage for 1,000 chickens.

For those of us with a smaller flock of 20 birds or so, it isn't practical to use the watering directions. So how do you administer the vaccine? The vaccine comes with directions. If you can't find them, you can get them from the company Web site. Two methods are of interest. The first is to use an included plastic dropper and administer one (very small) drop of vaccine into either the nostril or the eye of each bird. My birds are pretty tame. They jump up onto my shoulders to keep me company and have no real issue with me picking them up or handling them.

So in my case, this method works just fine. I set up a chair in the chicken yard and bring a couple of pieces of bread with me, and as each chicken takes a turn jumping up onto my lap, I gently hold its head still and beak closed and put a drop on one nostril. I then briefly close the other nostril with a finger until the drop gets sucked in, give the chicken a piece of bread, and send it on its way. But not all chickens are so friendly and cooperative. When I was a kid, we had some chickens who thought they were kamikazes or something, and securing their cooperation in such an endeavor was unlikely. So we vaccinated them through their drinking water. The question is how do you translate dosage instructions intended for 1,000 birds so they work for a small flock of 10-30 birds? Here's how I do it.

I rehydrate the vaccine in the vial using high-quality bottled water. I shake it thoroughly and then dump it into a 100 ml graduated cylinder. I add water to bring the total volume to 100 ml. Now I know that each milliliter has enough vaccine for 10 birds. I set that aside. Then I turn my attention to the waterer. I take it apart and clean it thoroughly with hot soapy water, rinse it thoroughly, and then dry it with paper towels. My water at home isn't chlorinated. If you have chlorinated water, do the final rinse with bottled water. Then, I put 1 gallon of bottled water, 1 teaspoon of powdered milk, and 1 ml of vaccine for every 10 birds into the waterer and stir it up.

Then I make sure that for the next 24 hours it is the only source of water available for the birds. The next day, I clean out the waterer thoroughly and then fill it up with my normal watering solution plus a vitamin supplement. The vaccines are live virus vaccines, and they put some stress on the birds, so I give them the vitamins to help them deal with that. Speaking of live viruses—I should mention that if you aren't careful while playing with this vaccine, you'll get a mild case of conjunctivitis—also known as "pink eye"—or maybe some coldlike symptoms. Nothing serious though. While I use this method for the Newcastle vaccine, it will also work for other vaccines that are dosed for larger flocks.

Antibiotics

Sometimes vaccinating chickens makes them sick, and they need medicine. Other times, they will get sick from germs you have brought home on your shoes from visiting someone else who has chickens or even from buying a couple of adult birds and introducing them to the flock—even if you keep them in a separated space for 10 days beforehand, which you should always do. This is a tough situation. If you are raising birds organically and they need antibiotics and you use them, the chickens are no longer organic—so you may be stuck destroying the birds.

Antibiotics commonly used for poultry. The most likely reason you would resort to antibiotics with chickens is respiratory illness. These sorts of illnesses aren't all bacterial—some are viral and unaffected by antibiotics. Nevertheless, I have found that most often the respiratory illnesses characterized by wheezing and nasal discharge or sneezing have all responded. Antibiotics will find their way into the eggs of laying birds, so the eggs should be broken and added to the compost pile during treatment and for a week afterward. The two most common antibiotics used for chickens are variants of tetracycline anderythromycin, both of which are available mail order or right in the feed store without a prescription. A study of tetracycline residues in eggs found that on the second day after finishing treatment, any residues in the eggs were undetectably low. 49 So disposing of the eggs for seven days following treatment is fine. On the other hand, while the meat is safe to eat one day following discontinuance of erythromycin, I have no data indicating that the eggs are ever safe to eat again. So laying chickens treated with erythromycin to cure illness should be transitioned into being meat birds and replaced with new layers.

As with vaccines, antibiotics are usually packaged in sizes suitable for much larger flocks, but a bit of math will let you know how much to use. One thing you will definitely need, though, is an accurate scale weighing in grams. Digital scales used to be quite expensive but can now be found for less than

$30.

Food

During the active growing season, birds will provide about half of their own food by foraging if the farmer keeps the size of the flock suitable for the area being foraged, but during the winter and for the first weeks after hatching, they will need to be given commercial feed. (The amount of pasture required per bird depends on the type of vegetation being grown in the area. Start with 300 square feet per bird, and adjust from there.) You can also feed grain and vegetable leftovers—such as bread and pasta—to your chickens.

Technically, you can feed them meat as well, but I would avoid the practice because too many diseases are being spread these days by feeding meat to livestock—things like mad cow disease that can spread to humans and is incurable. A small flock of birds will be much less expensive to feed than a house cat, and the feed is readily available at agricultural stores. A number of bird feeders are available commercially, or they can be built by the farmer.

Make sure that whatever you use for a feeder, it can be raised or lowered so that its lip is even with the backs of the birds. Building the feeder this way, and never filling it more than half full of feed will significantly reduce the amount of feed, that ends up on the floor since chickens have to raise their heads to swallow. If birds are used for pest control, a fencing system should be created that allows the birds to forage in and around beds that are sown with cover crops but not in beds growing food crops A small flock of birds will devastate a garden in short order because they like to eat most things that humans eat. They make excellent manure that should be added to the compost pile if gathered.

Otherwise, just leave it in the beds containing cover crops to naturally degrade and provide free fertilizer for the next growing season. Commercial feed comes in many varieties. Both medicated and nonmedicated versions of mash, crumbles, and pellets are available. If you specify it is for laying hens, the clerk at the store will know exactly what you need. The medicated versions aren't typically necessary. You can also buy a mix of cracked corn and rye called "scratch feed." Scratch is about half the price of regular feed but is not, in and of itself, a complete ration—although chickens tend to prefer it over regular feed. All feeds are very attractive to rodents, easily rotted by water, and a lure for grain moths, so they should be kept in metal storage containers with tight-fitting lids. One winter, I kept a feeder with both scratch and regular feed available in the coop for the birds that were confined while the snow was deep.

I also kept bales of alfalfa hay in the coop, covered with a tarp. Because the birds preferred the scratch to the complete ration, they became nutritionally deficient and sought to make up the difference by eating the hay. One of the hens developed an obstruction of her crop this way and had to be euthanized. So I have learned not to provide scratch while the chickens are confined, especially if an edible litter—like hay—is used.

Containers for keeping feed safe from pests. What we do instead, when the chickens must be confined because of bad weather, is provide a daily bunch of greens such as lettuce or kale to supplement their feed. This helps give the yolks a nice color and keeps the chickens from getting bored.

Housing

All birds have similar housing requirements though their habits are a bit different. A coop should be built for the birds with about three square feet of floor space per bird. Technically, as few as two square feet can be adequate for chickens, and ducks require only three square feet each, but the coop should be sized to account for temporary increases in flock size during the spring and summer. For a flock of 20 birds, which is the largest practical flock for a small lot, that means a 100-square-foot coop—a size that can be accommodated in a number of configurations such as 8 × 12, 10 × 10, and so forth. Enough floor space helps to reduce stress on the birds and prevents behavior problems.

The most prevalent behavior problem resulting from inadequate living space is chickens pecking each other, which can lead to infections and other problems. Nearly completed chicken coop. No matter which way you'd like to build a coop, I'd like to convey a few aspects of coops that I believe to be important. First, a coop needs to have a smooth floor, made out of plywood, for example, that is well coated with polyurethane or a similar substance that is impervious to moisture and easily cleaned or disinfected. The floor should be strewn with wood shavings, peat moss, or a similar clean absorbent material that is replaced anytime it becomes excessively damp or dirty in order to prevent infections. Some experts recommend against using hay, but that is precisely what we use without any difficulties as long as we don't store the hay bails in the coop.

Second, any windows should be made out of Plexiglas rather than real glass and preferably located high enough on a wall that the chickens can't get to it easily. That way they won't be tempted to fly into it and break their necks. Third, even the smallest omnivores, like mice and rats, can cause serious problems in a bird coop, so it is important to construct the coop in a fashion that will exclude even the smallest predators. The easiest way to achieve this is to build the coop on pilings. Finally, nests should be provided. These are most easily built onto the walls in such a way that the birds can get into them easily via the roosts and they are up away from the floor. Ducks, being more secretive, prefer a covered nesting box on the floor.

Nests should be filled with straw, wood shavings, or peat and kept clean. The farmer should provide half as many nests as there are birds. Because of the way the noses of birds are designed, birds cannot create suction with their beaks. As a result, they have to raise their heads to swallow. What this means in practical terms is that birds sling water all over the place and make the litter on the floor of the coop wet if the lip of a watering device is too low. If the lip of the watering device is even with the level of the backs of the birds, the mess created will be substantially reduced.

It is more important with some birds than others, and particularly important with turkeys, to make sure plenty of water is available anytime they are given feed in order to avoid choking. Water provided should be clean and free of debris, and the container should be designed to keep birds from standing in it or roosting on it. If birds stand in or roost over the water source, they will certainly contaminate it with droppings.

Adequate and comfortable nesting boxes are important.

Many books on poultry cover the lighting arrangements needed to maximize growth or egg laying. Light affects the hormonal balance in birds and therefore affects when a bird will molt (lose and replace its feathers), lay eggs, desire mating, and so forth. When birds molt, they temporarily stop laying eggs, which is a big deal on a commercial scale. Likewise, egg production naturally decreases as the amount of available light decreases. All of this can be affected by controlling the amount of light that birds receive and, to a lesser degree, the food supply. This brings up a fundamental difference in the mind-set of a minifarmer who is raising birds as compared to a large commercial enterprise. In a large commercial enterprise, the life span of a laying chicken is about 16 months because it has been pushed to its physical limits by that time and has outlived its usefulness in terms of the cost of food and water that it consumes compared to the wholesale value of eggs in a commodity market.

Likewise, because it has laid eggs daily without respite since reaching adulthood, the minerals in its body have become depleted and the quality of the egg shells has declined. So by the time a chicken is 16 months old, it is consigned to the compost heap because it isn't even good for eating. A mini-farmer can have a different outlook because the birds are multipurpose. The birds serve to consume pests and reduce the costs of gardening, consume leftovers, produce fertilizer, provide amusement with their antics, and lay eggs or provide meat for the table.

The economic equation for the mini-farmer is strikingly different, so the treatment of the birds will likewise be different.

If birds are allowed to molt when the seasons trigger molting and come in and out of egg production naturally because of seasonal light changes, they are subjected to considerably less stress, and their bodies are able to use dormant periods to recover lost minerals and nutrients. In this way, it is not at all unusual for nonspecialized bird breeds to live several years with moderate productivity.

A radiant heater behind the roosts keeps chickens warm in cold winter climates.

One other thing to consider if you live further north is the need for heat in the coop. Where we live, temperatures below zero are not uncommon, and there can be days in a row with temperatures never budging out of the teens. In these conditions, their water can freeze, and they can suffer frostbite. The water is easily dealt with via a simple water fount heater available at agricultural supply stores. For general heating of the coop, mine is insulated using thermal reflective insulation, and I've installed a simple 400W flatpanel radiant heater behind the roosts so the chickens can stay warm at night.

Collecting and Cleaning Eggs

Chickens usually lay midmorning, but there's no predicting it completely. They're chickens, after all, and lay when they are good and ready. Ideally, you should collect the eggs immediately, but this is seldom practical—especially if, like me, you work a regular job. I've never had a problem with freshness simply collecting the eggs when I get home from work and putting them in the refrigerator immediately. There are a couple of phenomena pertaining to eggs that may become an inconvenience: dirty and broken eggs. Every once in a while, chickens will lay an egg that has a thin shell and breaks while in the nest. Sometimes, they may lay an egg with no shell at all. When these break, they coat any other eggs in the nest with a slime that makes them unmarketable. Obviously, the proverbial ounce of prevention applies in that having enough nesting boxes will reduce the number of eggs coated with slime in any given box. However, chickens tend to "follow the leader" to an extent and have a decided tendency to lay eggs in a nesting box where another egg is already present. So even if you put up one nesting box for each bird, thisproblem wouldn't be solved completely.

Then, of course, there is the problem presented by the fact that eggs leave the body of a hen through the exact same orifice used for excrement. Meaning that sometimes eggs will have a bit of chicken manure on them. Not usually, but sometimes. In addition, chickens who have been running around outside in the mud on a rainy day will track mud back into the nest and make the eggs dirty. For minor dirt and manure, just scraping it off with a thumbnail or using a sanding sponge is fine.

But for slime and major dirt that won't come off easily, water washing is required. Water washing can be extremely problematic and yield unsafe eggs if done improperly. When the egg comes out of the hen, it has a special coating that, as long as it is kept dry, protects the interior of the egg from being contaminated by anything on the shell. But once the shell becomes wet, the semipermeable membrane of the shell can be compromised, and a temperature differential can cause a partial vacuum inside the egg that sucks all of the bacteria on the shell inside—thus creating an egg that is unsafe.

Farm-fresh eggs are easy to sell as they are qualitatively superior to even the best store-bought eggs.

Nevertheless, the techniques and technology for properly water washing an egg are very mature and well understood. Special eggwashing machines exist, but on the scale of a mini-farm, they are so expensive (about $6,000) they don't make sense economically. One alternative that I haven't tried yet is a product called "The Incredible Egg Washer" that sells for less than $120. But let me tell you about the safe and low-cost technique that I use for our small-scale operation.

First, clean your sink and work area thoroughly, and get a roll of paper towels so they are handy. Next, make a sanitizing solution from the hottest tap water by mixing two tablespoons of bleach with one gallon of water. You can multiply this by adding four tablespoons of bleach to two gallons of water, and so on. Put the sanitizer in a cleaned watering can and the eggs in a wire basket. Pour the sanitizing solution over the eggs very generously, making certain to wet all surfaces thoroughly. Wait a couple of minutes, and then use a paper towel that has been dipped in sanitizer to clean the egg. Use a fresh paper towel for each egg. Then, rinse them very thoroughly with sanitizing solution and then set them aside to dry on a wire rack. It's important to let them dry before putting them in egg cartons, because wet eggs tend to stick to egg carton materials.

The Broody Hen

Sooner or later, you are going to run into a hen who is very interested in hatching some eggs. If that is part of your plan— great! She'll sit on any egg, so take some others from adjacent nests that were laid that day, and slide those under her too. If, as in my coop, the standard laying nests are up in the air, make her a new nest that is closer to the ground—6 to 12 inches. That way, once the chicks are hatched, they won't hurt themselves if they fall out of the nest.

Usually, though, when a hen goes broody, you don't want it to happen. The hen will sit on the eggs, keeping them at a hightemperature, so that when you collect them a few hours later, they have runny whites and just aren't fresh anymore. Just collecting the eggs out from under her for a while won't work—she'll just keep setting forever. The solution to this problem is a "broody cage." A broody cage is any cage fashioned with a wire bottom and containing no litter. I've used a small portable rabbit cage for the purpose. If you keep a broody hen in this for 36 to 48 hours, it will break her of the desire to sit on the eggs. It is extremely important that you provide adequate food and water in the cage or you will force her to go into molt.

Chapter Six
Raising chicken for meat

A lot of people are squeamish about killing animals of any sort for food. Still others have moral or religious objections to the practice. If you have moral or religious objections, please skip to the next chapter as there is plenty of other information elsewhere in this book to help you raise a healthy diet without meat. If you are merely squeamish, though, this chapter may put you at ease. Be forewarned, though, that this chapter contains graphic pictures of chicken slaughter.

Selecting Chickens

For sheer efficiency, the easiest choice is to order day-old Cornish cross chicks from your local agricultural supply store. These are also known as "broilers." These are bred to grow quickly with lower feed requirements and to pluck easily. These are a sort of hybrid franken-chicken and are simply voracious eating machines. In fact, they eat so much and gain so much weight so fast that they may start dropping dead or breaking their legs from sheer weight anytime after 12 weeks of age.

Broilers gathered around a waterer. Another way to obtain chickens for meat is to let a couple of hens stay broody in the spring and raise a handful of chicks to broiler size by fall. Come fall, pick all the new roosters to be meat birds, plus any of the older hens that aren't laying, leaving yourself with a flock around the same size you started with in the spring—about 10 to 20. The meat birds get processed in the fall, vacuum sealed, and frozen. You should take newly hatched chicks and raise them in the brooder, and thenceforth keep them separate from your regular laying birds. Otherwise, your hens will figure out that you've killed them and get spooked, and your rooster will get aggressive.

Housing for Meat Birds

Unlike chicks of other breeds, broilers can usually be removed from the brooder at about four weeks old because they are pretty well feathered, and it's during a warm time of the year. This is good, because otherwise they'd outgrow the brooder. Regular layingbirds raised for meat should be kept in the brooder for six weeks before going outside. Meat birds are around for only three months of the year, at most, so permanent housing doesn't make as much sense for them as it does with laying hens. What a lot of small farmers use, and we use one too, is a device called a "chicken tractor." A chicken tractor is a portable enclosure that lets the chickens get fresh air and fresh grass. It is moved every day so the chickens don't end up lying around in their own excrement. There are about a million ways to make a chicken tractor. Just search on the Internet, and you'll find hundreds of designs, many for free. Your choice of design should allow for about four square feet per bird. Many designs are completely enclosed to exclude predators and keep birds from escaping. So far, I've had no real predator problems, and the Cornish crosses that we grow are too heavy to fly, so our chicken tractor is on wheels and has sides made of only three feet of chicken wire.

The easiest housing for meat birds is a chicken tractor.

Feeding Meat Birds

Meat birds should receive a starter/grower from the day they arrive until the week before they are processed. The week before, they should be put on a leaner ration. For this you can use either a finishing feed or ordinary layer crumbles like you give your laying hens. As broilers, particularly, seem to have a nearly insatiable appetite, you should feed them by weight according to the directions on the bag. Some breeds of meat birds will forage while in the chicken tractor, but the broiler crosses will mostly just lay around and eat feed. So you shouldn't count on forage providing a lot of their food.

Slaughtering Birds

Food should be withdrawn from birds destined for slaughter 12 hours before the appointed time, though continuation of water is advisable. This precaution will make sure no food is in the upper digestive tract and thus reduce the possibility of contaminating the meat with digestive contents.

A killing cone. They don't need to be this elaborate.

Usually, you should not carry a bird by its feet due to the potential for spinal damage, but for purposes of slaughter it is acceptable if done gently. Catch the bird by its feet and immediately hold it upside down. Swing it a little on its way to the killing cone, and it should settle down. Provide support for its back while carrying if needed. Then insert it head down in the killing cone. The proper way to slaughter a bird, except for farmers whose religions specify another method, is to cut off the bird's head while the bird is either hanging from its feet or inserted upside down in a funnel-type device called a "killing cone." Use a good, sharp, strong knife for this.

Put a leather glove on your weak hand, and grab the bird's head, holding its beak closed. Then, take the knife and cut off the head in one smooth motion. Once the head has been removed, any squawks or twitches observed thereafter are a result of patterngenerating neurons in the spinal cord and not conscious volition. I checked with my local veterinarian on this, and he assured me that cutting off the chicken's head is entirely humane. When the head is cut off, the neck will flex all over the place, splattering blood everywhere. I put a piece of Plexiglass in front of the killing cone to avoid getting blood on me. The bird should bleed out in 65 seconds or less, but it doesn't hurt to leave it for a couple of minutes because you don't want to scald a bird if it still has a breathing reflex because it could inhale water while being scalded. Hanging the bird upside down or using a killing cone is important for two reasons. First, it helps remove the greatest possible amount of blood from the bird's tissues, which presents a more appetizing appearance. Second, it helps keep the bird from struggling and hurting itself. 50 Blood collected from the bird can be added to the compost pile. If a killing cone isn't used, a noose can be used to hang the bird upside down by the feet.

A proper knife makes slaughtering easier.

A killing cone, mentioned previously, is a funnel-shaped device with a large hole on the top into which the bird is inserted headfirst. The hole in the bottom is large enough that the bird's head and neck stick out, but nothing else. The entire device is usually about a foot long. Killing cones can be purchased via a number of poultry suppliers, just be sure to order the correct size for the birds being killed. They are simple enough that anyone can make one from sheet metal and rivets, and many people have improvised by cutting the top off of a small traffic cone. Once the bird has been killed, it needs to be scalded and then plucked. In scalding, the bird is dipped and then moved around in hot water for 60 to 90 seconds to break down the proteins that hold the feathers in place.

Then, once the bird has been killed, grab it by the feet and hold it under the water for 60 to 90 seconds, sloshing it up and down slightly. The timing on this has some room for flexibility, so you can just count. If more than one bird is being processed, keep an eye on the temperature and add boiling water whenever the thermometer drops close to the low side of the recommended temperature range. The water should be replaced every dozen chickens, any time it has been allowed to sit unused for a half hour or more, or any time the water has obviously been contaminated with feces. In the case of broilers, this is usually for every chicken.

Once the bird has been scalded, the feathers are removed in a process known as plucking. It is easiest to hang the bird by its feet and use both hands to grab the feathers and pull them out. If the bird was killed and scalded correctly, this shouldn't take long, although it is messy. The feathers can be added to a compost pile and are an excellent source of nitrogen. A few small "pin feathers" will remain on the bird, and these can be removed by gently pressing with the back side of a butter knife. A few hairs will also remain, and these can be singed off by going very quickly over the carcass with a propane torch. If you process a lot of chickens, you might consider an automated plucker that is easily made at home.

The bird's entrails should now be removed in a process called evisceration.

1. Loosen the bird's crop, which is between the breast meat and the skin, by following the esophagus

down to the crop and loosening it. As you'll note, I wear disposable gloves for processing.

2. A sharp knife is used to carefully (so as not to puncture any intestines and contaminate the meat) make an incision from the vent in the skin of the abdomen up to the breast bone. There will likely be a layer of fat there, which you can carefully pull apart by hand.

Opening the abdominal cavity.

3. The viscera are carefully removed by hand. With the breast facing up, just reach your hand into the body cavity as far as you can.

Reach your hand deeply into the cavity.

4. Gently grab a handful of viscera, and pull it completely out of the body cavity. Then scrape the lungs off the backbone. (They are bright pink.) Some people save the heart, liver, and gizzard. If you do, separate them from the rest of the viscera and refrigerate them immediately.

You may need to remove a couple of handfuls of entrails.

5. Cut out the vent, being careful not to contaminate the bird with the contents. Use a garden hose to wash out the body cavity afterward.

Carefully cut out the vent.

6. Turn the bird on its back and cut off the neck. A lot of folks use the neck for making chicken stock, so if you do, it should be refrigerated immediately.

Put the bird on its back and cut off the neck.

7. Turn the bird right-side up and cut off the oil gland.

Don't forget to remove the oil gland.

8. Now, give the chicken a thorough inside and out rinse with the garden hose and put the completed whole chicken in a tub of

ice water. Make sure to keep an eye on the ice and keep it cold! I add a tablespoon of bleach (to kill germs) and a cup of salt (to pull residual blood out of the meat) to the water, but neither is strictly necessary. If you can keep the water ice cold for four hours before freezing the bird, it will be more tender than it would be if frozen immediately.

Monitor the ice water to make sure it remains icy.

Bird blood, feathers, entrails, and other parts can be composted just like anything else, although many books on composting say to avoid it. Many authors counsel to avoid animal tissues in compost because they can be attractive to stray carnivores and rodents and because in a casual compost pile, sufficiently high temperatures to kill human pathogens may not be achieved. But if you make thermophilic compost, the only precautions needed are to make sure that any big parts of the bird are cut up and that the parts are buried in the middle of the pile with plenty of vegetable matter.

In this way, the compost itself acts as a biofilter to stop any odors, and the high-carbon vegetable matter, combined with the high-nitrogen bird parts, will form seriously thermophilic compost in short order. Consequently, the nutrients that the birds took from the land are returned to the land in a safe and efficient manner.

Chapter Seven
Preserving your harvest

Since the aim of a mini-farm is to satisfy a large portion of your food needs, you should store your food in such a manner that it is available throughout the year. The four forms of food storage that I use and will describe in this chapter are canning, drying, dehydrating and root cellars. Many of these approaches have been applied in the United States for decades and can be introduced with confidence. Every approach has its strengths and disadvantages, which is why they are all shielded. Advanced methods that I do not clarify in this chapter include cheese making, wine making, and meat curing.

Canning Perhaps the most daunting method of uninitiated food storage is canning. Stories are heard of people dying from botulism because of poorly canned food, and some people believe that canning is an art like making fugu (a toxic Japanese blowfish) and that the slightest mishap would make canned food unsuitable. Fortunately, these experiences are not correct.

Modern canning methods are the result of decades of work and can be practiced by someone with a sixth grade education. (Yes, I knew someone actually with a sixth grade degree who canned safely.) A rare cases of badly canned foods resulting in botulism poisoning in the current age are from people who do not obey the most clear instructions about how to do so. Present requirements for home canning come from USDA work that is continuously revised.

Much of the criteria haven't modified for decades, so the analysis procedures are fairly comprehensive. USDA researchers deliberately inject viable heat-resistant bacteria spores into food in the home canning jars and then use temperature sensors within the jars while they are canned. After the canning, the cans are stored at the exact temperature required for the best bacterial growth for several months and then opened in a sterile atmosphere and inspected for bacteria or some other injury. The USDA standards published after the First World War allowed up to 2% spoilage, but the standards published since then require 0 percent spoilage. It ensures that food canned at home using current USDA standards is absolutely safe.

In addition, the times and temperatures given by the USDA do provide a safety factor. This indicates that if the experimenters had reached 0 percent spoilage at 237 degrees for 11 minutes, the criteria would require 240 degrees for 15 minutes. Hours and temperatures have mostly been measured up, never down. There are two types of canning: a hot water bath and a steam bath. The choice of approach depends on the level of acidity of the canned food. That is because the amount of time that spoilage species can live at a given temperature is greater in food that is less acidic.

So less acidic food gets canned using a steam pressure system that produces a temperature of 240 degrees; more acidic food gets canned in a boiling water bath that produces a temperature of 212 degrees. The amount of time defined for canning is dependent on how long it takes the heat to completely reach a given food in a specific jar. Standards for half-pint, pint, and quart jars are written. If a mixture (such as a stew) is canned, then the canning time and temperature for the entire mixture is dependent on that of the most time-consuming ingredient. By using the appropriate form, container and processing time, you can guarantee the health of your canned food.

Home Canning Jars Home canning jars are sold at Walmart and other hardware and grocery stores, but their supply is seasonal. These jars are thick walled and specially constructed to withstand the rigors of temperature, heat, and vacuum created by home canning. Forget about old-style (though attractive) jars with rubber gaskets and wire closures since they are no longer approved by the USDA. Today's specifications require two-piece caps that have a removable metal ring called a "crew" and a flat non-reusable cover that has a sealing compound along the outer lip.

The bands should be used once they are bent or rusted, but the lids will be thrown away after they've been used to buy new ones. Home canning jars are costly — about $7/dozen at the time of publishing. But expect a little more than $0.50 apiece. However, their longevity easily supports their cost — the home canning jars can last for decades. By the time the bottle had been used for 20 seasons, the expense had fallen to $0.02. If you buy jars and bands (new jars usually come with bands), you only need to buy new lids for each use — which are typically less than $0.10 each.

Food and Canning Methods The type of canning process required depends on how acidic the food is. Acid foods (with a pH of less than 4.6) requires only a water bath canning process, whereas less acidic foods (with a pH of more than 4.6) need steam pressure canning. Sadly, the mix of time and temperature in a pressure canner can make certain foods less nutritious and other foods less appetizing. Broccoli is a perfect example of how it takes such a long time of pressure canning to be healthy that the products are not worth consuming. Broccoli is best stored, either by freezing or by pickling.

The goal is therefore to use a system that preserves the optimum quality and palatability while retaining a reasonable safety margin. And if I don't recommend a canning process for a vegetable, it's because I've decided that it's best stored by some other process. An age-old technique for canning products that can not be easily canned otherwise is to improve the acidity of the fruit by either fermenting it or adding vinegar. Sauerkraut is a perfect example, since it is not appropriate for either canning or freezing in its fresh state, so if it is acidified by fermentation of lactic acid (and therefore called sauerkraut), it can be preserved in a boiling water bath while preserving the most essential health benefits.

(Technically, with great caution, you can freeze ground cabbage, although the results can vary.) Pickles are produced either by fermenting vegetables in brine (which improve their acidity by the creation of lactic acid) and/or through adding vinegar. These methods produce a sufficiently acidic liquid such that only a short period of time is needed in a water bath tub. Boiling water bath canning is ideal for all fruit, jams, jellies, preserves and pickles. Tomatoes are right at the edge of pH 4.6, meaning that they can be safely placed in a boiling water bath if a sufficient quantity of citric acid (or commercially distilled lemon juice) is added. The best sum is one tablespoon of lemon juice or 1/4 teaspoon of citric acid per pint. Alternatively, vinegar can be used at a rate of two teaspoons per pint, although it can induce off-flavors.

The acidity (or rather the flavor of acidity) can be substituted by applying two tablespoons of sugar to each tablespoon of lemon juice, which does not interfere with the canning process. Although few people chose to have figs (usually dehydrated instead), it is worth noting that they are right on the verge of acidity and that they will have lemon juice added in the same proportion as tomatoes if they are canned. All else — vegetables, beef, fish, and poultry — must be packed in a steam-pressure bath. Boiling water canners are free of repair.

Just wash them like any other dish, and you're done. Pressure canners, on the other hand, need limited maintenance. The accuracy of the dial gage on top of the canner should be tested annually by the Cooperative Extension Service. If this is erroneous, please give it to the supplier for re-calibration. If the canner is not in operation, stack it on top of the body with the lid turned upside down. Never immerse your lid or dial gage in the mud! Alternatively, clean them with a moist cloth and mild detergent if necessary. Clean the vent holes with a pipe cleaner. After through use, the rubber seal should be separated and washed with a damp cloth. Some vendors require that the gasket be lightly brushed with vegetable oil, and others do not — so make careful to obey the manufacturer's directions. When you follow the manufacturer's guidelines to use your pressure canner, it won't blow, as was often the case years before.

Modern canners have a range of built-in safety devices that our grandma's models ignored, and aside from intentionally undermining certain safety mechanisms, an accident is virtually unlikely. Foods to be canned are packed in hot glass jars using either a fresh pack or a hot pack process. Methods are fairly self-explanatory from their names: freshly packaged foods are put in the jars fresh and then hot liquid, brine or syrup is added, and heat-packed foods are put in the jars after they have been cooked. Any approach may be used in some situations. When sealed, the bottle is filled with liquid (brine, water, vinegar, pickling juice, etc. depending on the recipe) up to 1/4 or 1 inch from the top of the container.

This area is called the headspace and is required to support the expansion of food in the container when it is heated and to allow a successful vacuum sealing.

Using a Boiling Water Canner Boiling Water Canners come with a wire rack that carries the jars so that they do not rest on the bottom of the canner or crash against each other and split. Having a rack guarantees that the water at the same temperature covers the bottles on both sides and that the heating is equal and that the optimum results are obtained. The bottles need to be sterilized for the canning process.

Fruits Virtually any fruit can be canned, and all but figs are sufficiently acidic to be canned without additives. (Figs require the addition of one tablespoon of lemon juice per pint.) Fruit should be in optimum quality, free of noticeable blemishes or rot, and well washed. In order to be adequately heated during the canning process, the fruit that is larger than one inch will be sliced such that no single piece is larger than one inch square. Pits and stones of large-grained fruit should be removed, and the fruit should be handled in an antioxidant solution, particularly after it has been cut to avoid discoloration. Antioxidant products can be bought commercially, or you can make your own by mixing 3/4 cup of distilled lemon juice with a gallon of tea. Fruits are typically canned in sugar syrups because sugar allows the fruit to maintain its color, form and taste, while sugar is not purely required to avoid bacterial spoilage. If you prefer, the fruit can use plain water rather than syrup. I do not support the use of artificial sweeteners in syrup because saccharine becomes bitter from canning and aspartame loses its flavor. (If you have bought a diet of soda and felt it tastes a little like mud, that means the food was processed in a high temperature environment and the artificial sweetener was damaged.) The "very thin" syrup uses two tablespoons of sugar per cup of water, the "thin" syrup uses four tablespoons per cup of water, and the "medium" syrup uses seven tablespoons per cup of water. Attach the fresh-packed fruit to the bottles and then add the simmering syrup (or water) into the container until it is filled to within 1/4 inch of the bottom. Place the lids and the screw bands on the jars with your fingertips, then immerse them absolutely in a boiling water bath for the specified duration for that specific fruit. So remove the jars from the canner and let them cool for at least 12 hours. Hot-packed fruits are handled pretty much the same, except that the fruit is combined with the syrup and brought to a light boil, and then the fruit and syrup are added directly to the container.

Applesauce Home-canned apple sauce was my favorite as a kid — I'd crack a pair of home-made biscuits on my plate, add a decent amount of apple sauce on top, and dig in. Apple sauce canned at home is plain, delicious, rich and tasty — nothing like the homogenized items available in the grocery store. Naturally, the same method used for apple sauce may also be used for pears, quinces and other berries. Look free to play with it! Here's my secret and the process for semi-dry apple sauce. Yield: 22-26 pint Semichunky Applesauce 1 bushel of at least two varieties of apples, one of which is very sweet a bag of white and/or brown sugar (the exact amount included depends on your preference and the apples selected) cinnamon to preference all-spice nutmeg to taste lemon if desired Washing 3/4 of the apples and scraping the roots, chopping into 1-inch bits, including the core and peels, and pu

(You can buy a basic contraption for a few bucks that cores and slices apples into segments in just one motion — I highly recommend it!) Dive into an antioxidant solution until sliced. Cook until all the bits are tender. Start at high temperatures, then lower to medium-warm. Run the cooked apples through a strainer to extract the skins and seeds and put them back in the bowl. (You can make this hot if you're careful.) Peel and core the remaining apples, cut into small bits, and add them to the pot as well. (I have a "Back to Basics" Peel-Away apple peeler that peels, cores, and slices easily in a single process. It costs less than $20 at a cooking store.) Start cooking on medium-high until the freshly inserted bits are tender. Connect the cinnamon, lemon and seasoning to taste. You'll actually need less than 1/4 cup of sugar per pint if you've used any sweet apples. Reduce heat to a boil to keep the sauce hot while you can. Attach the sauce to the newly cleaned pint or quart canning pots, leaving 1/2 inch of the headspace. Place your fingertight on your lids and caps. Submerge the bottles of hot water in a boiling water bath for 15 minutes for pints or for 20 minutes for quarts. Enable the bottles to cool in a dry position for at least 12 hours before cutting the labels, marking and storage in a cool dry position for up to two years. Love it!

Jellies Jellies are made with fruit juice and sugar, which use heat and water to protect them. The distinctive consistency of the jelly is the relationship between the acids in the fruit, the pectin in the fruit, the sugar and the sun. Many fruits contain enough natural acid and pectin to create jelly without the need to add anything but sugar. They contain sour apples, crab apples, sour cane fruits, cranberries, gooseberries, grapes and currants.

Some fruits are somewhat deficient in acid, pectin, or both, and require a limited amount of additional lemon juice, pectin, or both. They contain ripe strawberries, ripe blackberries, wine grapes, cherries and elderberries. Finally, certain fruits obviously won't make jelly without adding a large amount of lemon juice and/or pectin.

We contain strawberries, apricots, plums, pears, blueberries and raspberries. Since sugar plays an essential role in the survival of jellies, the quantity needed for the recipe should not be decreased. It also plays an important role in the manufacture of the drug gel, such that the use of too little sugar will lead to syrup instead of jelly. The juice used to produce jelly can be processed in a variety of ways. If you are using a juice machine, using it only for fruit that will also need additional pectin, such as bananas, plums and pears.

That is because the juice system does not remove pectin from high-pectin fruits properly. The typical way to remove the juice is to clean and cut the entire fruit (it is necessary to keep the peels on as the pectin is stored near the peel) and to position it in a flat bottom pot on a stove with added water. For soft fruits, using only enough water to avoid scorching, but for hard fruits like pears you may need as much water as a pound of fruit. The fruit is cooked over medium heat until it is tender and then squeezed into a jelly jar. When you choose a crystal-clear liquid (which I don't really care for, but other people find esthetically important), it's important not to pinch the jelly jar, but rather to let the juice flow through naturally and gradually. You're expected to get around a cup of juice per pound of fruit.

Jelly bags of varying sizes can be bought from grocery retailers and over the Internet. When you are using a juice pump, the resulting juice will always be filtered into a jelly bottle. When you can't find jelly packets, you can use a double sheet of cheesecloth filled with a colander instead. Until the juice has been drained, it is mixed with sugar and other ingredients (e.g. lemon juice and/or pectin, depending on the recipe) and heated on the burner until it reaches a temperature of 220 degrees, as determined by a candy thermometer. The boiling point for pure water is 212 degrees, although this boiling point is increased as certain ingredients, such as sugar, are added to the bath. If the water evaporates and the proportion of sugar in the water decreases, the boiling point will rise gradually.

If you live in the mountains, deduct 2 degrees for every 1,000 feet above sea level. So if you stay at 3,000 feet, deduct 6 degrees — then heat the mixture until it exceeds 214 degrees. This is because the higher you are above sea level, the harder it is for water to evaporate due to lower air density. Once the appropriate temperature has been achieved, fill the sterilized jars with a hot mixture up to 1/4 inch from the rim, place the two-piece caps on the jars with a fingertip, and heat the half-pint or pint size in a boiling water canner for five minutes.

Brined Pickles and Kraut Pickling preserves food by raising its level of acidity. It is used for foods that are not naturally acidic enough to be safely canned using a boiling water method. The two methods most widely used are lactic acid fermentation in brine, and infusing with vinegar. Brine fermentation is most often used with cucumbers to make kosher-style dill pickles, but it is also used to make sauerkraut. Many other vegetables—like collard greens—can also be processed this way.

There are three very important aspects of doing brine fermentation. First, keep everything clean. Second, use only plain salt with no additives whatsoever, or all sorts of cloudiness and discolorations will result. (Regular salt contains anticaking agents that will make the brine cloudy as well as iodine that will inhibit proper fermentation. Use canning salt!) Finally, pay close attention to the correct procedure, or your pickles will be soft and possibly even slimy. Brine fermentation can take several weeks.

It is also temperature sensitive and works best at temperatures ranging from 55 to 75 degrees. Before starting brined pickles, make sure you have both the time and the space to leave the containers undisturbed for a while. You should only use glass, nonchipped enamel, or foodgrade plastic containers for fermentation. Under no circumstances should you consider using a metallic container because the product will become contaminated and possibly even poisonous. Don't use old-fashioned wooden barrels because sterilizing them is practically impossible. Start off with well-cleaned containers and well-washed produce.

Brined Dill Pickles

5 lbs of 3- to 4-inch pickling cucumbers 3 heaping Tbsp whole pickling spice 8 heads of fresh dill (1/3 of a bunch) 3/4 cup white (distilled) vinegar 1/2 cup pickling salt 5 pints (10 cups) of clean pure water The proportions of salt, vinegar, and water in this recipe are not approximations—measure them exactly! You can double or quadruple the recipe if you keep the proportions the same for a larger batch of pickles. Put half of the pickling spices and a light layer of dill in the bottom of a clean food-grade plastic pail or pickling crock. Put in the cucumbers. Mix the remaining dill and spices with the salt, vinegar, and water and pour over the cucumbers. If the amount of liquid isn't enough to come about two inches above the cucumbers, make more liquid from water, salt, and vinegar according to the same proportions. Take a clean plate and place it on top of the cucumbers so they are held completely under the brine. The plate may need to be weighted down with a second plate. Cover the container loosely with plastic wrap covered with a clean towel held on with a couple of bungee cords tied together around the container like a big rubber band.

Try to keep at room temperature—certainly no warmer than 72 degrees and no cooler than 60 degrees. Uncover and check the pickles for scum once a day. Use a clean spoon to scoop off any scum, then put the towel back on. This should be the only time the pickles are uncovered. After three weeks, check the pickles by removing one from the container, cutting it lengthwise, and tasting it. If it is translucent and tastes like a good dill pickle, you are ready to can the pickles. If not, wait another week and try again. Once the pickles are ready, remove them from the brine and pack into cleaned and cooled glass jars with a couple of heads of dill added to each jar. Take the brine, pour it into a large saucepan, and bring it to a boil, then pour it over the pickles in the jars, leaving

1/4-inch headspace. If you run out of brine, make additional brine from 4 pints of water, 1/4 cup of salt and 2 cups of vinegar raised to boiling. (Again, proportions are exact rather than approximate— use measuring cups!) Put the lids on finger-tight, and process 10 minutes for pints or 15 minutes for quarts in a boiling water canner. Yield: 10 pints.

Sauerkraut Cabbage Canning/pickling salt

Any sort of cabbage can be used for this recipe, but larger heads tend to be sweeter. Remove any damaged outer leaves, quarter the heads, and remove the hard cores, then weigh the cabbage on a kitchen scale. Weighing the cabbage is important because the weight determines the amount of salt to use—3 Tbsp of salt per 5 pounds of cabbage. Shred the cabbage into slices of about 1/8 inch thickness, and using clean hands thoroughly mix the cabbage with the salt. Put the mixture into a five-gallon food-grade plastic container a little at a time and use a clean potato masher to mash the mixture until enough juice has been squeezed out of the cabbage that at least one or two inches of juice are above the cabbage by the time all the cabbage has been added.

Fill and seal a noncolored food-grade plastic bag with a mixture of 6 Tbsp salt and one gallon of water, and put this on the cabbage to weigh it down and keep it completely submerged, then cover the top of the container with plastic wrap. Keep the container at room temperature, and in four weeks, your sauerkraut will be ready. Just like with the brined pickles above, check daily for scum and remove any that you find. Once the kraut is ready, pour it in a large pot (or a portion of it at a time depending on the relative size of your pot) and heat while stirring to 190 degrees as indicated by a candy thermometer. Do NOT let it boil. Pack into clean canning jars and add brine to leave 1/4 inch of headspace, and process in a boiling water canner for 15 minutes for pints or 20 minutes for quarts. Yield: depends on how much cabbage you use.

Quick Process Pickles

Quick process pickles rely on vinegar for their acidity rather than fermentation, so they are faster and easier to make. (And you needn't worry about scum!) The vinegar used to make pickles lends its own character to the pickles, so be cautious about using flavored vinegars such as red wine, cider, or balsamic vinegar unless specifically required in a recipe. When the type of vinegar isn't mentioned in a recipe, use white distilled vinegar. The preservation process relies on a certain specific amount of acid, so always use vinegar that is 5% acidity.

Bread and Butter Pickles 4 lbs cucumbers, washed but not peeled 3 thinly sliced medium onions 1/3 cup of canning salt 4 cups distilled vinegar 3 cups sugar 2 Tbsp mustard seed 1 Tbsp + 1 tsp celery seed 1-1/2 tsp turmeric 2 tsp whole black pepper Slice the cucumbers 1/4-inch thick and the onions as thinly as practical. Combine all of the ingredients except the cucumbers and onions in a large sauce pot and bring to a simmer (not a boil!). Add the cucumber and onion slices, and bring to a very light boil before turning down the heat to low. Pack the slices into jars and then fill with pickling liquid to 1/4 inch headspace, and put the lids on the jars finger-tight. For the most crisp pickles, pasteurize by placing the jars in water deep enough to be at least 1 inch over the top of the jar lids that is kept at 180-185 degrees (check with a candy thermometer) for 30 minutes.

Alternately, you can process in boiling water for 10 minutes for either pints or quarts. Allow to sit six weeks before using for the development of full flavor. Yield: 4 pints.

Vegetables

Vegetables (other than tomatoes) are not acidic enough to be canned using the boiling water method. Instead, they must be processed in a pressure canner for a fairly long period of time. The process is essentially the same for all vegetables, the only difference being in the processing time. For larger vegetables, cut into pieces so that there is at least one dimension less than 1/2-inch thick, bring pieces to a boil in water (to which 1/2 tsp of salt per quart can optionally be added), pour hot into clean jars allowing the right amount of head space, put on the caps finger-tight, and process for the time.

You might consider using a little sliver (1/2-inch × 1-inch) of kombu kelp instead of salt. Kelp enhances the flavor of canned vegetables because of the natural glutamaic acid that it contains. Generally, the pressure canning methods employed with vegetables destroy a good portion of the vitamin C, so I recommend freezing instead. Regardless, the macronutrient and mineral values of vegetables remain intact after canning, so it is worthwhile if you don't have a freezer or reliable electric service.

Meat

Meat is usually better vacuum sealed and frozen, but where the electrical supply is unreliable or too expensive, canning meat is a viable alternative. Because canning times and temperatures for meats are significant, most vitamins that can be destroyed by heat, especially vitamin C, are destroyed in the process. On the other hand, both the protein and mineral value is unaffected, so as long as you have plenty of vegetables in your diet, canned meat isn't a problem.

While the USDA says that putting raw meat into jars and then processing it is safe, it is my opinion that the flavor suffers. So I recommend that all meats first be soaked for an hour in a brine made with 1 Tbsp salt to a gallon of water and then at least lightly browned in a little vegetable oil until rare and then packing into the jars. Once the meat is packed into the jars, the jars should be filled with boiling water, meat broth, or tomato juice to leave the amount of headspace described in Table 19 . Most people prefer 1/2 tsp of salt added per pint, but this is optional. Put on the lids finger-tight, and process for the appropriate length of time. You can season meats before canning them, but avoid sage because the prolonged high temperatures can cause bitterness. Also, any meat broth you u s e shouldn't contain flour, corn starch, or any other thickening agent because under pressure canning conditions, thickening agents congeal and make it impossible to get all of the air properly evacuated from the cans, and the risk of spoilage is increased.

Soups, Stews, and Other Mixtures

When canning anything that is a mixture of more than one ingredient, the time and headspace requirements from Table 19 that are the longest and largest for any of the ingredients apply. So if, for example, a mixture of carrots and peas were being canned, the processing time and headspace requirements for peas would be used since those are the greatest. The same warning about thickening agents regarding meats applies to stews as well.

Buffalo Stew 4 lbs buffalo stew meat cut into 1-inch cubes 12 medium red potatoes cut into 1/2 inch cubes 5 medium yellow onions, diced

2 lbs of carrots sliced 1/4-inch thick 2 stalks celery 1 Tbsp cooking oil 1 tsp salt 1/2 tsp ground black pepper 1 tsp thyme 1 clove garlic 3 quarts water Get the three quarts of water boiling in a large saucepan and brown the stew meat in oil in the bottom of another large saucepan. Add all of the spices and vegetables to the meat, stir thoroughly, cover, and allow to cook down for five minutes. Then pour in the three quarts of boiling water

slowly and carefully, and bring everything to a boil. Put into jars leaving 1 inch of headspace, and process in a pressure canner for 75 minutes for pints or 90 minutes for quarts. Yield: 9 pints.

Freezing

Like canning, freezing has its pros and cons. In its favor is that it is easier and quicker to freeze vegetables and meats than it is to pressure can them, and the resulting product is usually closer to fresh in terms of quality. Some things, like broccoli, are just plain inedible when canned but perfectly fine when frozen. The downside is that when freezing an appreciable amount of food, a large freezer is required—which isn't cheap. Figure at least $300 for a new one at current market price. Also a consideration is the ongoing everincreasing cost of electricity. And, if you are in an area prone to long electrical outages, you could lose the entire contents of your freezer if you don't maintain a backup power supply of some sort.

So you'll have to weigh the advantages and disadvantages. We have a reliable electric supply and not a lot of spare time at my house, so we do a lot of freezing. I used to freeze in regular freezer bags from the grocery store or wrap things in freezer paper. No more! Now, the only method I use, and the only method I recommend, is vacuum sealing. Vacuum sealing consistently yields a superior product that keeps up to five times longer, so it is what I'll describe.

Getting a Sealer

It may not be practical to wait around for a sealer to show up at a yard sale while harvest season comes and goes—but it never hurts to look. There is another big reason why these sealers end up in the yard sale bin: the price of bags.

There are two suitable sealers on the market in various configurations available at department stores—the Seal-a-Meal and the FoodSaver. I've found both to be adequate, though you will find the FoodSaver a bit more expensive. I prefer the Seal-a-Meal since its design allows it to work better with a wide variety of bags. These are light-duty home-use units. They work fine for the amount of freezing that I do for the carbohydrates and vegetables for a family of three because we tend to freeze in relatively small batches of 10 or fewer packages at a time. Heavy-duty commercial units are available—but you should hold off on these until you see if the lessexpensive home-use units will meet your needs. Certainly they will work fine as you ramp up for the first couple of years.

First, keep an eye out for the sealers and bags at yard sales.

Second, use plastic rolls instead of premade bags because by cutting them to size for what you are freezing, you will use a lot less and save money. Finally, you can buy bags and rolls from brands other than those made by the manufacturer of your sealer. Two sources come to mind. First, a number of manufacturers make less expensive bags and/or rolls including Black and Decker, FoodFreshVacstrip, and Magic Vac.

These usually cost less than half of what the other bags do. Second, check the Internet. There are eBay stores dedicated strictly to vacuum sealers that offer good deals and also Web sites dedicated entirely to getting good prices on bags, such as vacuum-sealerbags.com. With these resources in hand, you will see the superior properties of vacuum sealing become financially viable.

The Freezing Process Freezing is a six-part process that requires harvesting, blanching, cooling, drying, sealing, and freezing. First, since no form of food preservation can actually improve the quality of food, harvest as close to freezing time as possible, and thoroughly clean the produce. Hose it off with the garden hose outside first, then put it in a big bucket to soak that contains two tablespoons of salt per gallon of water to draw out any insects. Then cut it up as needed, rinse out the salt, and weigh it into portions using a kitchen scale. For vegetables, figure 4 ounces per person. So for a family of four, you'll want your bagged portions to be about 16 ounces, or 12 ounces for a family of three.

Weighing produce for consistent portions helps with menu planning. Next comes blanching. Blanching serves to inhibit the enzymes that destroy the quality of food in storage. There are two common methods—placing the produce in boiling water for a period of time, or steaming it for a slightly longer period of time. Both methods work, but I recommend steaming because it preserves more of the vitamin content of the food. The blanching time varies depending on what is being frozen. When the allotted blanching time has passed, the produce should be dumped into a bucket of ice water so that it is cooled down immediately. (I slip a metal colander into the bucket first so that it holds the produce and makes it easy to retrieve.) Leave the produce in the ice water for the same amount of time as it was being blanched, then take it out and put it between a couple of superclean, dry, and fluffy towels to pat dry. You have to do this when vacuum sealing otherwise the large water content gets in the way of making a good seal.

Dehydrating

Drying food is one of the oldest methods of food preservation. By removing most of the moisture from foods, enzymatic action and microbial growth are retarded, and the food will keep for a long time. Food loses more nutritional value from drying than from freezing, and dehydrated foods will seldom reconstitute with water to look like appetizing fresh produce. But even at that, dehydrated products make a conveniently stored, tasty, and healthy addition to soups, stews, and sauces. Just like vacuum sealers, dehydrators run the gamut from inexpensive units available at department stores costing less than $50 all the way to commercial-sized behemoths. I recommend starting with a small model that includes a fan and thermostat since that will be easy and trouble free. You can always switch to a more expensive commercial or even homemade unit later.

You can use a dehydrator for fruits, vegetables, and meats, though the process for the three is somewhat different. Vegetables destined for the dehydrator need to be cut in slices no more than 1/4 inch thick and blanched just as though they were going to be frozen. This helps them dehydrate better and keep longer. Fruits should also be sliced no more than 1/4-inch thick andthen dipped in a solution containing one tablespoon lemon juice per quart of water before being put in the dehydrator.

Fruit shouldn't be blanched. Every dehydrator is different in terms of its drying characteristics, so use the drying times and temperatures recommended in the literature that comes with your particular model. Meats, especially ground meat and poultry, are problematic because dehydrating is not the same thing as cooking, and the temperature seldom gets high enough to ensure pathogen destruction. This becomes an issue because bacterial contamination of these meats is common, so failure to thoroughly cook them can result in serious illness or even death. There are some jerky mixes available at department stores that are specifically formulated to deal with potential contamination of ground meats through the use of nitrites. If you choose to use one of these mixes, follow the directions precisely! Outside of this exception, I don't recommend making jerky or dried meat from either ground meats or poultry. Other meats—like beef steak/roast, venison, buffalo, and so forth— are perfectly fine. Most jerky recipes are for raw meat. In recent years, a number of universities have done studies and concluded that the practice could no longer be considered safe, and that meat for jerky should be precooked in a boiling marinade. With the foregoing in mind, then, here is my general-purpose jerky recipe.

Chapter Eight
Selling your produce

The mini-farm achieves its first economic advantage by raising enough food to reduce family food bills. During the first two years of mini-farming, the family is likely to use everything that can be made. Yet in the third and following years, it is possible to reduce food bills and sell enough food to offset employment as the two economic factors are put together. Growing enough food to reduce food bills is quick, but the thought of selling food looks like a bear at first glance. And, of course, it's a bear because you imagine attempting to convince the nearest branch of the multinational grocery chain to purchase your items. It's impossible to succeed, even even if it did, that would be a poor idea, because you'd be dealing with multinational companies using vast economies of scale and below world wage labor, and you wouldn't make much money.

It is important to note that, even as there are places where a mini-farm is at a disadvantage relative to agribusiness, mini-farms have incredible strengths that offer a strategic edge as well. The biggest agriculture area at the moment is organic growth. The organic mark has come to such a degree that even big department stores are selling it. The concern is that, even with this growing trend in chemical-free goods, large companies have taken action and have started to drive local producers out of the market. Yet it's not just gone.

Large-scale agribusiness organics suffer from many of the same problems as traditional products — especially problems associated with long-distance transportation, pre-maturity processing, and selection of varieties for shipment rather than flavoring. This is where the small farmer has an insurmountable advantage on the market, as the small farmer will specialize in varieties picked for flavor and deliver naturally ripened goods that have not lost their nutrient quality in the factory for two weeks. Locally grown organic heirloom vegetables and herbs are highly appealing to locally run supermarkets, convenience shops, restaurants and natural food outlets, not to mention neighbors! There are other benefits that derive from the fact that mini-farms run on a small scale.

A mini-farmer may speak to the owner of a nearby health food store or restaurant and enter into an arrangement to grow different crops. The big warehouse can't do that. Mini-farmers can also grow labour-intensive crops that are immune to automation and where the energy of the farmer can yield a superior output. In fact, specialty crops can be picked. Specialty crops, such as purple potatoes or rare lettuce, do not make sense on a wide scale in agribusiness, but they can find a ready audience through farm stands, small shops and restaurants.

The "Bigest Little Farm in America" is using this method to raise $238,000 on only 1/2 acre of land. In light of all this, it is no wonder that the number of small farms is rising at a rate of 2%

each year and is expected to continue to increase at that rate for as long as the next 20 years! Sales to retailers will, of course, be at wholesale rather than retail prices. This lowers the profit margin, but has the bonus of a ready market. Restaurants and neighbors — by selling to the restaurant or setting up a farm stand — represent retail rates.

The downside is that it could be tough to get business from restaurants and farm stand profits are unpredictable, but the advantage in terms of higher profit margins warrants consideration. Folks who are apt to find mini-farming may have trouble recognizing themselves as salespeople, but selling the produce is somewhat different from other forms of sales. First of all, you're selling everything you've built with your own hands and you're proud of it. Second, you're offering stuff with an incomparable nature.

Finally, instead of attempting to build an unrealistic demand, you're offering what everybody wants. As a consequence, this is something that should be done with a sense of moral dignity in the spirit of a genuinely mutually beneficial agreement. Approaching the local restaurant owner or the owner of a small health food shop is not difficult as you already have what these people want: excellent produce from a local manufacturer. Marketing and public relations interest of the use of fresh vegetables, and local produce has excellent flavor and nutritious content so long-distance shipment is stopped. The aim is clearly to bring forward a solution that reduces the burden on the part of the owner and encourages reciprocal benefits.

The biggest threats to the local restaurant and health food shop are the loss of stock where it is needed and the procurement of items that either can not be sold or will harm their reputation. This latter problem is allayed by the availability of samples and the continuous distribution of the best quality materials. The first consideration calls for a little thinking. As a single small field, a mini field has no size to defend against crop failure, freak hail storms, and the like. Notwithstanding the best hopes, a mini-farmer just can't guarantee an unfailing supply. Likewise, a supermarket or shop of a modest scale would sell much more produce than a mini-farm would be able to deliver in the best of seasons. The alternative is to make it clear to consumers that they plan to fulfill no more than 20% of their demands, ensuring that their existing partnerships with larger vendors remain unchanged. In this way, you're going to be able to sell anything you can make, so your buyer has no costs. This basic technique works incredibly well.

New and Approved Agricultural organic foods produced without toxic insecticides, fungicides or fertilizers have a premium quality of about 40% more than traditional goods. It is also important that organic cultivation should be viewed purely from the point of view of marketing, not to mention the environmental aspects.

The use of the word organic for food products is limited by federal law in the form of the National Organic System. The bottom line is that if the gross profit from cultivation is less than $5,000 a year, a farmer may use the term to apply to goods as long as they are genuinely produced in compliance with the plan requirements. If the gross profit is more than $5,000, there would be substantial licensing costs and a great deal of documentation is required. The costs are usually on a sliding scale — meaning 'the more you produce, the more they take.' A mini-farm is expected to be making less than $5,000 in gross profits annually, and having organic labels at the beginning is entirely feasible; if that mark is reached, certification funds should be considered a cost of doing business.

Even then, it helps to search around for a USDA-accredited rating provider whose fees do not cover all earnings! Many State Divisions of Agriculture are approved by the USDA, which is the least costly path. Alternatively to the expense of the National Organic Plan, Certified Natural Grown is a free initiative that meets the same standards but does not have any accompanying costs. Certified Natural Grown is targeted for small local growers and features stringent checks to allow for simplified paperwork requirements.